CAN THIS CHURCH LIVE?

CAN THIS CHURCH LIVE

A CONGREGATION, ITS NEIGHBORHOOD, AND SOCIAL TRANSFORMATION

DONALD H. MATTHEWS

The Pilgrim Press
Cleveland

DEDICATION

This book is dedicated to my five children:
Big Jon, William, Joanna, Little Jon and Faith.

May their children see the Promised Land of
Brown v. Board of Education.

The Pilgrim Press
700 Prospect Avenue East
Cleveland, Ohio 44115-1100
thepilgrimpress.com

Published 2004.

08 07 06 05 04   5 4 3 2 1

Library of Congress Cataloging-in-Publication Data

Matthews, Donald Henry, 1952-
    Can this church live? : a congregation, its neighborhood, and social
    transformation / Donald H. Matthews.
        p.   cm.
    Includes index.
    ISBN 0-8298-1648-8 (paperback. : alk. paper)
        1. Community—Religious aspects—Christianity.   2. Church renewal—
    United States.   3. Race relations—Religious aspects—Christianity.   4. United
    States—Race relations.   I. Title.

BV625.M28   2004
261.8'0973—dc22

                                                        2004053352

Contents

■■

Acknowledgments

■■

FIRST, I WOULD LIKE TO EXPRESS my gratitude to the church members who allowed me to observe them in their time of crisis and challenge. I made friends who I hope will remain lifelong friends, even if only in my memory. I would like to thank my daughter, Faith, who was my running buddy for a year of fun in the sun. I also thank my eldest son, Jonathan, who was an able babysitter and confidant. Willie and Jon continue to amaze me with their achievements. And Jo, perhaps anticipating the vision put forth in this book, gave me a "white" son-in-law, John.

I continue to draw intellectual strength from James Gustafson, the most gifted of ethicists in the United States and from the eminent Catholic theologian, David Tracy, for his vision of plurality that is still a challenge for our churches. I owe many thanks to my Berkeley seminary professors: Archie Smith, Durwood Foster and Charles McCoy. Charles and Archie introduced me to the work of H. Richard Niebuhr, and Jim Gustafson finished the job.

This text is more autobiographical than my previous writings. For this I need to thank those persons who gave me a vision of a church without barriers. My thanks go to William and Jackie Vance, Lela and Ron Harper, Donald and Brenda Guest, Roger and Joyce Hatch, Doug and Becky Cunningham, Ted and Helen, Phil, Nancy, Liz and Pete, Rev. Ardith, Amy and Dave Nelson, Alene, Liz, Scott, Peggy, and the Social Concerns Committee; Lee Price, Yetta Kilgore, Martha Hoaglund, Liza, Lisa, Chris and Ulrike, Joyce Williams, Jeremiah Wright, Sam

Beene, Virgil and Maggie Gage, Thee, Dwight, Thabiti and Angell, Steve and Rosie, and Kenneth Smith. These are just a few of the persons who taught me about the marvelous diversity that God has created.

The American Studies Department at the University of Santa Cruz allowed me the time, space, and opportunity to conduct this research. Their hospitality was greatly appreciated.

A special acknowledgment is extended to my family. My siblings, Mary, Carole, Alvin and William; my nieces and nephews, Annie, Tracy, Gerald and Lisa; and my uncles and aunts, Doris, Johnetta, Martin, Wade, Bill and Thomas, for being there in times of need. My ex-wife, Joanna, continues to challenge me to excel.

My mother, Ada Beatrice Welch Matthews, passed away during the writing of this text, yet I felt her presence and encouragement in every way possible. She now rests with the great line of African American, Mississippi spiritual blues women who have made our family strong. I miss you, Mom.

Finally, I would like to thank my administrative assistant, Deborah Foster, for her hard work and my editor, Kim Sadler, for her oversight and vision. Ms. Sadler had the patience of a saint, the determination of Hagar, and the wisdom of Sheba.

A special thanks goes to my copy editor, Cindy Karcher, for helping me make the rough places smooth.

Introduction

■

THE PUBLICATION DATE FOR THIS book is fifty years after one of the most celebrated Supreme Court cases in the history of race relations in the United States. Fifty years ago, the Warren-led Supreme Court abolished the doctrine of separate but equal in the case of *Brown v Board of Education, 1954.* Although the case was concerning the desegregation of public schools, it had a tremendous impact on all facets of life in the United States. The Supreme Court's interpretation of the Fourteenth Amendment, which guaranteed among other things due process and equal protection under the law, led to the dismantling of hundreds of years of state-enforced segregation of public institutions. However, the hope that this ruling would result in an end to segregated schools in particular, and racist institutions in general, has not yet become a reality.

Regardless, this was an important milestone in American history, and its subject matter, racial relations between whites and non-whites, is the main topic of this book. It is important then to recognize the historical legacy of *Brown* and the continued quest for a just society fifty years after the decision. It is unfortunate that fifty years after the decision, we are still struggling with the problems of racism and discrimination in our private and public lives. Instead of the formation of a more integrated society, we are faced with a situation of resegregation, or voluntary segregation, as whites continue to move from geographical and educational spaces that are becoming populated with persons of color. White men in particular continue to avoid marriage with non-white women. The lack of interracial marriages continues to reinforce the caste-like status of race in this country. This fear of miscegenation was an underlying fear of the white community that *Brown* did not address. Eventually, white Americans will have no further place to go and the problems posed by a multi-ethnic and multicultural society must be faced head-on by a generation of Americans with no place left to hide and very little guidance about how to achieve a caste-free society.

This text will only examine a small but important segment of American life–its churches–in regard to this problem of racial segregation. Chapter One will set the tone with various autobiographical reflections on my encounters with mainline churches in the United States. I have purposely avoided including an overwhelming number of statistics to "prove" that American churches are racially and economically segregated. The statistics exist for the curious, and most of us experience that lack of integration in our weekly worship services.

Chapters Two and Three discuss the situation of one church in particular that will be used as a case study of a church in the midst of social transition. It examines some of the processes and procedures used to guide the church in this process of social and congregational change. The roles of various persons, from church consultants, lay leaders, to pastoral leaders, are discussed as they grapple with the future of the church.

Chapter Four discusses two churches that successfully made the transition from a homogenous church to a more culturally-diverse church. Analysis of these churches will identify some salient points for church leaders who are in the process of negotiating this transition.

Chapter Five presents a readily accessible series of questions and exercises that church leaders can use in leading their churches through a time of transition. Church members should be encouraged to participate in these exercises as a way of acknowledging their strengths and weaknesses for becoming a church that welcomes change and transition.

Chapter Six presents the results of a ministry project in which middle-class churches were aided in developing ministry programs for children and families in their communities. This work was supported by the Carnegie Corporation of New York and the Chicago Theological Seminary. These programs can serve as outreach tools for churches who wish to be more inclusive of persons and families from lower economic levels in their community.

Sometimes the universe is kind and allows you the blessing of knowing if you are on the right track. I received a gift from the Spirit quite recently while I was in the midst of completing this book. Two incidents occurred that were due much more to grace than to chance and reaffirmed my purpose for writing this work.

The first incident occurred when, out of the blue, I was approached by the largest church in this region concerning the racial status of their church. Even though they had gone through a tremendous surge in their congregation, several of the members were concerned that the membership was virtually all European American. This was a point of concern for them for two reasons. First, it did not match their vision of what a church that called itself Christian should look like. Second, the church would eventually stall and begin the slow slope to decline if they continued to only draw from a discretely-numbered European American populace. They had formed a committee to investigate this state of affairs and asked me to serve as a consultant as they began to deliberate over this concern.

I met with two of their representatives and gave them some initial guidance to understand their situation. They followed up on my suggestions. Presently, they are in the process of developing further contacts and strategies to deal with their situation before it becomes a crisis with which they will have very little control.

The second moment of divine embrace occurred in Chicago, Illinois during my fiftieth birthday celebration. I don't mind mentioning my age, if you, my reader, can know that I have not only gained knowledge, but some wisdom as well. One of my oldest friends at the celebration is now a church official in one of the largest Protestant denominations in the country. It was his task to supervise a number of churches of varying ethnicities in a geographical region that covered the inner-city of Chicago and its integrated suburbs. He was an African American pastor whose credentials in the Civil Rights movement were impeccable. He had come a long way from being a Sunday School teacher in an all black church on the south side of Chicago. On one particular Sunday, he visited one of the churches in his area that had a long-standing policy of racial segregation. The church was on the verge of closure as many of its members had died or left for greener pastures. As he walked into this old and venerable church to conduct its annual meeting, he heard several of the members quietly whispering to each other, "There goes that nigger superintendent."

He was not shocked by what he heard but he was dismayed that this church that was on the verge of closure due to their inability to become receptive to its increasingly diverse neighborhood, still hung onto its traditions of racial segregation. As he told me the story, we were both amazed at how this church clung to its outdated social policy despite its impending end as a church. In fact, after this particular meeting, the denominational officials decided that this church could not be saved and it was slated for immediate termination.

These two instances served as divine reminders for this project. Even though this problem has affected the European American church the most, other churches will also face the problem of racial inclusiveness as their neighborhoods face social and economic transition. More than one predominantly African American church has been affected by the movement of middle-class African Americans to more affluent neighborhoods, leaving behind the poorest of the poor and those least likely to become members of a predominantly middle-class church. Although black churches have tended not to flee their neighborhoods, they still face the challenging need to minister to and develop supporting ministries for poorer members of their community.

I remember the speculation of one of my seminary professors who believed that the Jonestown tragedy was possible because the black church had not developed effective strategies for reaching the poorer members of their communities. The majority of those who died in Jonestown were poor people of color who believed and followed the preaching of Jim Jones. The black church, asserted my professor, had left a vacuum of ministry and mission that Jim Jones filled, regretfully, to their shame and tragedy.

Many African American churches in low-income neighborhoods also find themselves in communities that are undergoing gentrification—the process in which property values climb because more affluent European Americans purchase and rehabilitate property in inner cities. Will these churches simply ignore the influx of European American persons in their community like their predecessor European American churches, or will they attempt to develop a church membership and mission that is racially and class inclusive?

   All authors' perspectives are ultimately influenced by their biography; mine is no different. Some might ask why a professor of African American religion would be interested in the topic of European American churches and their prospects for ministry. Growing up in the ultra-segregated south side of Chicago has left an indelible impression on my soul and spirit. When I was old enough to realize that my racial classification would stigmatize and handicap me, I was puzzled as to why this was so. How can a society that claims to have the most democratic government of any society enact laws, policies and mandates that affect my status as a person of color? Today, the question that first puzzled me as a ten-year-old child still remains unanswered as an adult. It remains unanswered because as an adult, my race continues to affect my status in life.

   After I became a Christian and began to take seriously its philosophy concerning the unlimited grace and love of God for all peoples, this question only intensified. How can a society that claims to be the most Christian of all societies allow racism to become a functional and entrenched part of its social fabric? Much of my research both here and abroad has been an attempt to come to grips with the development of African American culture and religion under the burden of racial oppression. Therefore, it is only natural that I shift the focus of my thought and research on those persons and institutions that have benefited from and been the agents of this institutionalized practice.

   Unlike most black or white scholars, I have spent much of my life as a church person in both black and white church contexts. In my early childhood, I was a member of the African American Baptist and Methodist churches. My young adulthood was spent as a member of the European American Southern Baptist and United Methodist Churches. It was in these institutional bodies where I was licensed and ordained to the ministry. My educational formation was influenced by the white conservative as well as liberal religious bodies, both that had problems coming to grips with the problem of racial segregation and separation.

Upon deciding to study the sociology and psychology of religion at the Pacific School of Religion, the Graduate Theological Union at Berkeley and The Divinity School of the University of Chicago, I became affected by scholars who had been influenced by the great Neo-Orthodox theologians of the first half of the twentieth century—those being H. Richard Niebuhr and Reinhold Niebuhr. The work of H. Richard Niebuhr is especially important to this study. His work gave me a broad categorical template from which I could speak about the relationship between religion and society. Although H. Richard Niebuhr had little to say about issues of race and racism, his brother Reinhold was prophetic in his prediction that African Americans would one day use their spirituality to foment a social transformation of their circumstances.

H. Richard Niebuhr's ethical framework, which begins with an injunction to ask, "What's going on?" sounds simple but it is an amazingly profound dictum for it requires the ethicist to utilize the tools of the social sciences and humanities in his/her investigation of the topic at hand. This question requires the investigator to consider all sides of an issue and how various forces are at work in shaping social and personal practices and attitudes. What Niebuhr called "the fitting response" to ethical issues is impossible to identify without a thorough knowledge of how the problem was created. We are therefore moved beyond opinion to the consideration of evidence and ethical norms in the formulation of the strategy to achieve the desired goals.

Christian institutions in the United States have yet to develop the fitting response to the question of racial segregation in the church in part because it has yet to develop a fitting response to racial issues in the larger society. The European American majority population of the United States continues to feel threatened and intimidated by persons of color because of social policies such as Affirmative Action. The numerous incidences of racial profiling and the continual challenges to affirmative action in the courts speak to this great distress and concern. At the same time, its institutions have yet to come to terms with the effects or meaning of two hundred years of slavery and one hundred years of historically state-sanctioned discrimination. The social effects of slavery and discrimination continue to provide the limits for black upward mobility as blacks find themselves bereft of capital and other resources that European Americans have taken for granted.

Mahatma Gandhi once asked the black mystic and theologian, Howard Thurman, why blacks persisted in being Christian since Christianity had such a bad record in solving issues of race and racism. In fact, Western Christian countries had been the authors of social policies based on the linkage of Christianity with notions of white supremacy and civilization. Thurman found himself speechless, once again leaving me with an opportunity to consider this situation.

The livelihood and Christian identity of European American churches will eventually depend on how it deals with this issue. As this nation continues to grow in its populace of people of color, there will be fewer and fewer communities where European American Christians can live that will be void of the presence of people of color. And even if the European American church continues to live in its segregated form, will it truly be the church or a glorified version of what the church should be? If the church can live, let it live as it was intended at its birth on the morning of the first Pentecost—multiethnic, multicultural, gender empowering and class free!

CHAPTER ONE

The State of Mainline Churches

∷

C HURCHES SHOULD BE THE BACKBONE of our neighborhoods. They are often the indicators of the health and well-being of our neighborhoods whether or not we are talking about our downtown areas or the suburban sprawl. Many of our churches are faced with the challenge of declining church membership. Others have members but have no effective ministry. This chapter will be a readable and accessible overview of the issues faced by the mainline churches in a variety of neighborhoods.

I will discuss the social reasons that lay behind the crises that face membership in mainline churches which have led to the rise of mega-churches and alternative spiritual movements. The thesis of this chapter is that mainline church membership has been declining due to a failure to adapt to a new cultural situation. Even more importantly, many churches are not fulfilling the purpose of their existence. Later chapters will argue that the purpose which should be affirmed in the church is to be the transformers of personal and social life.

Many American churches are faced with the decisions of their lives. Will we live or will we die? Additionally, the question of what kind of ministry is to be equated with life must be addressed. It is the thesis of this book that the question of "Will we live or die?" is a question of will, as in having the will to live, and it is also a question of who is included in the "we." Having the will to live means facing up to the hard facts of American history and its decisions concerning who is involved in the word "we." Recent scholars and theologians have talked about pluralism as the very foundation of Christian theology but the inclusion of persons from different cultures has been a difficult task for European American mainline congregations to digest.

How a church decides to answer this question will have a great effect on its ability to thrive under conditions that are difficult or just downright intimidating. It seems that most American churches have answered this question in a way that has limited their viability. They have made decisions that have required little of them for the sake of comfort or expedience. In the name of a truncated view of their community, these churches have been encouraged by church and denominational officials to develop churches that are homogeneous. This is done for the sake of expediency, since according to denominational experts, it is easier to grow churches with persons who are alike. Even though congregations in the United States have expressed a desire for inclusion and diversity, this call has not resulted in any measure of success. The latest data shows that 90 percent of Christians in the United States worship in congregations that are less than 10 percent inclusive of other racial or ethnic groups.

In the birth of America's European American churches, churches were often very little more than ethnic enclaves. These Christian churches were ethnic communal organizations that were organized around their European nationality more than any idea of an inclusive community that cut across racial or ethnic lines. As these churches were faced with the presence of other European American ethnic groups and later, black and other non-European American persons, they most often made the decision that reinforced their ethnic heritage. This required little will or courage and the church became captive to ethnic and racial relations that were based on ideas of European American supremacy and manifest destiny. Their community lines, their sense of who their "we" was, stopped short of inclusion of non-European American persons. Richard H. Niebuhr's landmark study, *The Social Sources of Denominationalism*, revealed that Americans developed their churches along social factors that reflected their European ethnic boundaries. Recent studies also reveal that only 7.5 percent of congregations in the United States are racially mixed and half of those are mixed due to temporary demographic shifts.

American churches became captives of the racial and ethnic sensibilities of racial prejudice instead of the gospel of Jesus Christ. This limited theological and ethical stance led to hundreds, if not thousands, of white churches simply closing their doors when faced with racially-changing neighborhoods. These churches simply locked their doors and followed their European American membership to the suburbs or to wealthier communities.

Preachers and church leaders rarely stood up to the efforts of real estate speculators and racist demagogues who fed on the racist fears of the American populace. Instead of insisting that their churches become anchors against white flight by fighting against the blockbusting efforts of real estate and bank speculators, church officials dreamed of building bigger and better churches in neighborhoods that did not have the challenges of racial and ethnic diversity.

This white flight, which characterized the development of churches in the last century, has continued as the primary dynamic of church and neighborhood relationships. This strategy is obviously short-sighted and short-lived. Ethnic minorities have gained middle-class status and with this status bought houses and rented apartments in those areas that were once European American enclaves. And now, with the high cost of gasoline and the inconvenience of spending an exorbitant amount of time commuting to and from jobs in major urban areas, European Americans are now returning to the cities. They are reclaiming neighborhoods that were once thought to be blighted, and of course, too ethnic to be attractive to European American middle-class, upwardly mobile Americans.

We now find that European Americans have come full circle through the process politely called "gentrification," and are returning to the urban core. They have found that there are numerous economic opportunities in returning to the city, but more importantly, that there are few places where they can now live to avoid the presence of ethnic minorities. Many European American laypersons welcome diversity and see the church as the place where the vision of Pentecost, a place of ethnic and cultural diversity, can be attained. Despite their desires, however, they find little in their cultural history to suggest that this is a real possibility in their particular situation. They understand all too well that their churches were founded during a period of white flight and that racial attitudes, and more importantly, racially-defined cultural behavior, are difficult to change.

Along with the natural inertia that sets in with any kind of organization, the average European American church finds itself seduced, threatened, and in competition with the mega-church movement that has taken America by storm over the last twenty years. Everyone wants their church to be the next mega-church, including pastors and church leaders. Mega-churches offer themselves as the model for the perfect church. They have offered classes and courses to their less fortunate brethren as to how they, too, can become the next mega-church in their own community. They seem oblivious that their growth is due to the benefits of certain sociological conditions rather than solely due to some divine intervention and spiritual plan that anyone can learn and activate for their own church.

They also fail to realize or they discount how much their mega-churches are built on the same principles of exclusivity that led to European American flight in the first place. I remember being a seminarian in a conservative Christian church in the late 1970's when the mega-church phenomenon began. Those persons who were pushing the mega-church process were very much aware that they were advocating a model of church growth that was based on homogeneity rather than diversity.

They reasoned that it was more important to reach as many people for the gospel than to practice a gospel that was a model of Pentecost. Homogeneity as a principle of church growth, which plainly stated, meant recruiting persons of the same ethnic and class status, was more important than developing churches that were diverse, loving communities of faith. The development of multicultural and multiracial churches, they argued, was much more difficult and their studies showed that they simply did not grow as fast as churches that emphasized sameness.

So just as European Americans moved to suburbs to avoid non-whites in the urban core, they were now encouraged to only recruit European American persons of their same ethnic and class situation. The will to develop churches that were reflective of the community was once again replaced by what was easiest for the sake of a "we" that was the smallest common denominator. Perhaps this is why the American church has little moral authority in a society that continues to suffer from racial and ethnic separation and distrust.

Racism and the Church

While writing this chapter, I remembered an occasion while I was in graduate school that bore directly on this topic. I was asked to attend a meeting of pastors who were interested in dealing with the issue of racism in their churches. Most of the pastors in the group were European American and their churches were located in the white ethnic neighborhoods in the racially-segregated south side of Chicago.

After attending several of the meetings, it became obvious that the pastors were stumped as to how to address the issue of racism. The African American clergy, I among them, related how our pastors and church leaders would often preach on the necessity of love, and as a mark of a Christian, especially loving the enemy. We related how this preaching even occurred during the tumultuous sixties when black youth were venting their anger against the larger white society. Despite the presence of police brutality and racial injustices of many kinds, these black churches never wavered in their teaching and preaching of love.

When African American clergy asked the European American pastors what prevented them from giving the same message of love to their congregants, the European American pastors were in accord as to why this was impossible. They asserted that the preaching of love for blacks would result in the immediate withdrawal of support for their pastorate and, most likely, their dismissal. Since most of these ministers were appointed to their positions and not elected, I was amazed at the fear that these ministers had of their congregations. They were convinced that racism was so deeply embedded in the souls of their congregation that any attempt to preach racial equality and tolerance would be unsuccessful.

It will probably be of no surprise to anyone that this group soon disbanded. It became obvious that the lack of pastoral leadership would doom any attempt to change the racial attitudes of their churches. Due to the pastors' refusal to risk the ire of their congregations, there was little hope that their membership would be willing to participate with persons of different ethnic groups. I understood and conceded that these pastors were making accurate assessments of their congregations' attitudes and therefore, I didn't take the severity of their situations lightly. However, without strong leadership, change is next to impossible as we shall see in the case study to come. My experience in the black church reveals that there are at least two leadership styles. One is the pastor-led church, and the other is the Deacon or Trustees-led church. In the case of the white pastors mentioned in this section, they were protected from their congregations by virtue of their being appointed through an appointment process in which the church is consulted, but the decision to appoint is made by the Bishop and his/her Cabinet and, therefore, they had less to fear from the typical Protestant church in which those decisions are made by the congregations. Regardless, the pastor is a religious leader and must be held accountable for his/her leadership decisions.

To illustrate my familiarity with such a situation, I will relate what happened when I was a member of a predominantly European American congregation in northern California. My family and I were the only African Americans in the congregation. The church was located in a working class community that was comprised mostly of middle-class European Americans with a growing Latino and African American population.

The church was a middle-sized church that was built by its members. Several of the European American males had married Latino women but these women's ethnic heritage was seldom lifted up. They were viewed as extensions of their husbands rather than as persons who came from a different culture. I joined the church because of the paucity of trained African American clergy in the area. I also genuinely liked the pastor and respected his sermons that revealed a high level of education and an openness of spirit.

I won't relate everything that happened to me in that situation but I will relate that this congregation eventually licensed me to preach and sent me off to seminary. Before I left the congregation, I had an exit interview with the pastor of the church. The pastor related the many calls he received from the members when I joined the church three years before our interview. He stated that these callers were convinced that I was an undercover agent for the Black Panther Party and that the Black Panthers had sent me there to disrupt the church.

Besides thinking that these persons had a heightened feeling of their own importance, I was astonished at the depth of the distrust that accompanied my presence at the church. After all, I was a teacher at a school not more than four city blocks from the church. I had attended the best educational institutions and I was just as zealous as they were about my Christian faith. To the pastor's credit, during our time as members of the church, he never bothered me or my family with this information. He allowed the congregation and my family to get to know and respect each other on our own terms. Unlike the pastors in the Chicago meeting, he could have been removed by a simple vote of the church, yet he served as a buffer between the negative racial attitudes of his church and my family. This pastor was also open to worship with neighboring black churches and initiated several joint congregational worship experiences. However, he was advised by denominational advisors that the best way to "grow a church" was through a philosophy of homogeneity in which churches grew by trying to attract new members that were of the same ethnic and class status. I remember listening to these church growth leaders and the pastor as they presented the plan for growth for the church that was to be based on the ideal of racial and class sameness. This church eventually dwindled to less than fifty members. It found new life, however, when in its desperation it called a pastor who insisted that they follow his vision of a multi-ethnic, multicultural church. Three years later the church had grown to almost four hundred members, and whites were now less than twenty percent of the church, a percentage which was more reflective of the community's white population.

While I was at the church, I never presented to the congregation a person who wasn't true to my views on American racism and the suffering of ethnic minority people. For instance, when I was interviewed by the Deacon Board, which served as the screening committee responsible for granting licenses to clergy, I was asked about my political views–views which were decidedly to the left of the general congregation. I answered truthfully, and found that even though they disagreed with me, they stated that they knew that I was sincere in my beliefs and that they recognized the gifts of the Spirit in my life.

In this situation, leadership made all the difference. Other members of the congregation slowly began to be affected by the pastor's openness to persons of different cultural perspectives. This pastor was not afraid to address the issue in his sermons and in personal counseling sessions with his congregation.

The pastor at this church was unable to get the congregation to be open to the cultural styles that were already present in its own membership. In this case, the pastoral leadership was ready for change but the denominational officials could not arise beyond their social conditioning to embrace growth through embracing diversity. The pastor of this church soon left and the congregation began its downward spiral toward oblivion. Young persons who wanted diversity were turned off by attitudes that were developed in an America where segregation was the law of the land. The children and youth of the congregation became frustrated with those leaders in the church who sought to develop an all European American enclave. They would see and experience diversity in their schools and workplaces and wonder why it could not happen in their church, the one place where diversity should be the rule and the norm.

Unfortunately, this was also during the time when the homogenous church growth movement was at its peak. As this congregation thought about its mission, it was led away from embracing ways in which they could live within an increasingly diverse community by denominational officials. They, therefore, continued to emphasize racial and economic homogeneity.

At the same time that this church was grudgingly trying to change its attitude, another much younger church not more than a mile away would become the first mega-church in the area. Led by an African American pastor who had a vision of racial and ethnic inclusion, he developed a congregation that put into action the ideals of racial and class inclusion.

I am not writing this work simply as a disinterested sociologist or psychologist of religion. My experiences as a black layperson in predominantly European American churches has given me a unique perspective on what the European American churches can be if they are willing to open themselves to diversity.

One of my most powerful experiences was as a layperson and Sunday school teacher in a predominantly European American and conservative Protestant evangelical church. One of my European American friends and I were concerned that the church was not reaching out to all persons in the community. In order to help change this situation, we formed a Friday night Bible study that was open to church members and persons in the community who were seeking a place of fellowship.

After several weeks, we soon began to develop an interracial attendance of adults. We then formed an evangelism team. Each Thursday night, my friend and I would meet in prayer and under the guidance of the Spirit, visit persons we knew in the community whom we felt had a need for spiritual guidance and/ or a church home.

On one occasion we visited a Hispanic family who became members of the Bible study group. This family began to feel comfortable in our multicultural setting and decided to attend the church. This was significant because both the wife and husband had grown up as victims of racism. They regularly met European Americans with racist attitudes and were subjected to racially derogatory remarks from the majority of the European American community. The fact that they were willing to try and become a part of our congregation was a testimony to the closeness they felt with us as we shared our lives together in our visits and weekly Bible study. Our willingness to share our lives in prayer and study became the basis for Christian fellowship.

However, when they attended the church they felt the same alienating spirit that they had grown up with in their community. The European American members of the church, even though they stated that they wanted a church that was open to the community, could not hide their discomfort with the new additions to the congregation. Despite our encouragement, it was not long before they left the church and we eventually lost touch with them and their family.

In another instance we found that the church began to challenge the evangelism we were conducting. The sight of a black man from the inner city of Chicago and a European American guy from the deep South in partnership was too much for many in the church to accept. Our motives were questioned and we were suspected of trying to build our own church. The pastor of the church endorsed our efforts and cooler heads prevailed.

Despite these suspicions, we were led one Thursday to witness to the husband of one of our Bible study attendees. Even I had little hope that we could reach her husband since he was the stereotypical hard-drinking, hard-working, truck-driving good old boy. Much to my surprise, when we began to share the gospel with her husband, he began to be moved emotionally and spiritually. He was soon crying and asking for God to be a part of his life. In this most personal of moments I realized that the power of the Christian gospel was to be found in this meeting of disparate spirits over mutual concerns of the meaning of life and death. His wife, of course, was overjoyed and it wasn't long before he made his way up the aisle to give his life to Christ for baptism.

The pastor of the church took great delight in informing the church of the process by which this man came to become a part of the church in the hope that the congregation would realize that it was possible to develop the church as an interracial fellowship. The pastor even asked my friend and I to stand with the new convert as he made his confession of faith and joined the church.

Still, the majority of the church refused to let go of their skepticism and I realized that if they couldn't be moved by the sight of a highly educated black man standing in fellowship and friendship next to a good old boy from a humble Southern background, then nothing else would move them from their spiritual inertia.

It is these incidents in my life that have left me curious as to the process of decline in European American churches. I have been a member of black and European American mainline Protestant churches in small and large cities in America. Because my wife is Catholic and I have taught in Catholic institutions of higher learning, I have seen some of the same processes at work in Catholic churches as well.

I don't believe that this decline is inevitable. I refuse to believe that the only alternative is to give in to the lowest common denominator of homogeneous church growth. The Spirit of God is not confined by class, caste or race and neither should the church reflect these same restrictions. Churches with the proper leadership can overcome their circumstances, especially if they are open to coming to terms with their cultural isolation. Churches that are willing to change, and by churches I am really emphasizing church leaders, can change but only if they can come to grips with some often painful and deep-seeded cultural attitudes that have existed in the social fabric of the United States since its inception.

Instead of small churches wishing to be mega-churches or giving in to alternative spiritual movements the church can make a stand by preaching a gospel that is inclusive and prophetic. Many persons are attracted to alternative spiritual movements because they feel as though the mainline denominational churches have lost their spiritual center. After living in such diverse communities as Rochester, New York; Santa Cruz, California; Philadelphia, Pennsylvania; Kansas City and St. Louis, Missouri; and Chicago, Illinois, I have seen the American populace reject the church, while at the same time, they have thoroughly embraced God as a spiritual presence.

I recall that during my days in a conservative Christian seminary there was one professor who was a hold out to the idea of growing churches by inclusion of diverse peoples in the urban core. He taught courses in religion and society and what was then called Applied Theology. He gave his students insights into the possibility of the church actually becoming representative of diverse people under the overarching banner of Christianity and what it stood for at Pentecost. Several of his students went on to minister in churches that were in poor black and brown communities. They were not the norm, however, as it seemed that every seminarian wanted to have a church like Robert Schuller or a ministry that would reach thousands of persons just like themselves.

It is a subtle psychology that teaches church leaders that they have a responsibility to the world to reach all people on earth and convince them of the truth of the Christian gospel, yet also emphasizes the necessity of an exclusivist ministry. The Christian church was inclusive at its very beginning. We forget that it was a diverse church that comes to us in four gospels and there were twelve disciples and several women who formed the core of Jesus' ministry.

Alternative Spiritualities

Americans are very inventive regarding the expression of their spirituality. Even the ministers of mega-churches, most of who in reality preach a very traditional and conservative Christian message, have adopted a style that is countercultural to the culture that is expressed in mainline denominations. The mega-church ministers know that there are many persons who are dissatisfied with the traditional Protestant church and even though they have a similar message, they have removed any signs of traditional Protestantism from their preaching and worship environment. Much of their success is found in their verbal critique of the traditional church. In a society which revels in negative ads and mudslinging in politics, those in mega-churches have found that traditional churches have given them copious material to criticize Christians and spiritual seekers who are searching for an authentic spiritual expression.

Persons who first attend these "contemporary" services are surprised at how these churches combine a critique of culture with a cultural style that is reflective of modern culture. The preaching style is highly personal and conversational as opposed to the traditional robed and elevated, hierarchical position of clergy in the traditional churches.

The music in mega-churches is a combination of contemporary music with a Christian message. It is more akin to a highly polished stage show complete with highly accomplished soloists and musicians who know how to play to the emotional needs of the audience. Interestingly enough, this is a style that was first developed by the black church in decades of gospel music workshops and church experimentation. Black gospel musicians were among the first to realize the power of using contemporary gospel music to reach a mass audience. The heavy dose of music that speaks to the heart and core of one's spirit is of great appeal to a populace that experiences the bureaucratic life of modern society as oppressive and stultifying. Church leaders who realize this have been particularly successful in attracting and keeping new membership.

The accoutrements of the traditional church are removed. There are no large crosses or stained glass windows with pictures of Christian martyrs. The emphasis is on the present. These churches are often modeled after that most modern of American structures, the mall. Often there are food courts and informational booths in wide open spaces that are directly styled after the mall. The cultural disjunction presented by traditional European architecture, modeled after a Gothic or colonial style, gives way to the modern mall and building complex. In other words, those structures and styles that would remind parishioners of the failed spirituality of middle America, are removed.

It is these lived experiences and observations that I brought with me to what I will call Old Church–the church I will describe in the ensuing chapter. In attending this church, I was soon to get a view of a declining church at its moment of decision. This gave me an opportunity to reflect in a more disciplined manner, the immense possibilities of church transformation.

The United States continues to exist as a highly segregated society. American neighborhoods continue to be racial and ethnic enclaves which prevent the easy and effective intermingling of culturally different individuals. There, however, is also the process of European Americans returning to inner city areas to take part in the revitalization of the inner cities. African Americans, Asian, and Latinos/Latinas continue to move into higher income levels. They can now afford to move into neighborhoods that once excluded them from membership. Younger persons are growing up without the deep-seated prejudices of their foreparents who grew up during the time when segregation was still the law of the land.

Schools and places of employment are becoming increasingly integrated. God's Church has a unique opportunity to put into place the diversity that has marked the workplace. Additionally, the church can put those same ideas of equality and respect into action in their ministries. It is not enough that persons be forced to work together by laws of social policy. The key to a truly healthy society will come when peoples' hearts and minds are transformed. This is the job of the church, not the government, the school or the workplace. This is the challenge to which this book is directed. Let the church live!

CHAPTER 2

The Situation of Church A

■■

THIS CHAPTER WILL DISCUSS THE history and present situation of Old Church. It will describe the major turning points in the life of the church which led to its present decline. I came to be a member of Old Church during a leave of absence from my job as a sociologist at St. Louis University. I was looking forward to teaching and completing some research in a distinguished department of American Studies at a venerable state university. I soon found myself searching for adequate housing and found a place to stay in a church parsonage with the pastor of Old Church. Old Church was experiencing many of the problems that have afflicted hundreds, if not thousands, of mainline churches.

Old Church was founded in the middle of the twentieth century. It was the beneficiary of an influx of first and second generation American families who were moving into the area where the church was located, before the proliferation of modern suburbia. It was during a time of city building, before malls and sprawling apartment complexes. Old Church was the initial church of its denomination in the area. It was to become the flagship of the churches in that area, representing all that the denomination wanted its churches to be in a fast-growing metropolitan area. It was a growing church, full of young families with enough children and youth to make a full religious education plan a necessity.

Old Church was located in a neighborhood that was in the middle of downtown. It was close to the prominent shops, stores and offices of the city. It was close to the public library and the City Hall. It soon became a landmark and reference point of the city. Old Church, with its steeple and its majestic architecture, was the place where you could guide others to in and around the downtown area.

The worship space was huge and an educational building would be built to deal with the overflow of children and youth that would soon come to inhabit the growing neighborhood. Persons who strolled the downtown area on weekends and during their lunch hour would be attracted to the grounds of Old Church and read the signs announcing their welcome for worship and Christian education. If space was important in the life of the church, then Old Church was in the perfect place for growth and ministry.

The church and the growth of the town were inseparable. The town was growing slowly into a bustling metropolis and the church was growing right along with it. This was the time of middle Americana when drive-in movies and drive-in restaurants were new inventions. It was before the sixties when the very nature of a town such as this would be questioned. Old Church's leaders simply had to do the job they were appointed to do. Preachers preached, teachers taught, trustees passed the plate and collected and counted the money with no thought that there would not be enough to care for the church's expenses.

The church, like the town, was predominantly European American. It took its identity from a citizenry that saw itself as defenders of the American way of life. Most of the town and church members saw themselves as the benefactors of an America that gave them hope of a better life than the one they had left in Europe. In the United States they could realize their dreams of success and wealth. Many of them had fought against fascism in World War II and communism in the Korean War.

They were not critical of a country that was borne out of the colonization and exploitation of American Indians, Africans, Mexicans and Asians. Most of them and their families were not Americans during the height of this domination and exploitation. They only saw the present and its opportunities.

The city and county had a large population of Latino/Latina laborers who toiled in the nearby orchards and farms. They were invisibly present to the European American members of Old Church since they lived on the outskirts of the city. The children of Old Church rarely encountered them since the children of migrant workers seldom enrolled in the same schools. It wasn't until high school, after the racial boundaries had become realities in the customs and attitudes of the town, that European Americans and Latinos/Latinas intermingled. Those persons of color who lived in the community were often domestic workers who lived in the small cottage houses directly behind their employer's house. Some also commuted by public transportation to serve in the homes of their more affluent European American neighbors. They lived on the fringes, the margins, and even though they were inhabitants of their county long before the European American majority had arrived, they were now distinct minorities–in power and in numbers.

The lay leadership of the church was made up of men who were also the civic and business leaders in the community. It was not unusual for town officials to use their membership in Old Church as a steppingstone to political life. Church was as much a civic commitment as it was a spiritual duty. Community leaders were expected to be prominent actors in the life of the church. This kind of religion, termed *Civil Religion* by some, made few distinctions between the American way of life and Christian practices and beliefs. This was Christianity without a social critique. The culture and the religion of Old Church were in sympathy with each other. The sermons, the Sunday school lessons, and even the large cross which hung prominently in the sanctuary were reinforced by the American flag. Life was good and there was no need to be concerned by what or who was not present in the life of the church.

As I spoke to long-time members, former pastors and others who were familiar with the life and history of Old Church, a pattern began to emerge that was to be repeated in congregations across the country. The advent of the Civil Rights movement began to disturb the self-satisfaction that was previously experienced by many members of Old Church. The attitude of cultural isolation was no longer the dominant attitude. Racial and ethnic minorities began to assert their rights to live and work in any neighborhood in the United States. Several members of Old Church were sensitized to the problems of racial and class exclusion and began to lobby for social change inside and outside of the church. The downtown neighborhood which was once all European American was now experiencing racial change as Latino/Latina and new African American immigrants began to move into the community.

The specter of integration meant that Old Church members would begin the pattern of European American flight that would lead to the expansion of cities to suburbia or to higher income communities within the city. Those with money began to leave the Old Church downtown neighborhood and find residences that would surpass the old neighborhood. The lay leadership did not experience an immediate change because the old leaders continued to attend the church—even though they had to travel fifteen minutes instead of five minutes to church.

There were those among the congregants who were often spurred on by younger, more idealistic pastors, who challenged

Old Church to minister to those who were moving into the community. Old Church was challenged to become a truly multiethnic congregation but they were without a road map to make it happen. Not only were they up against their own ignorance of other ethnic groups, they faced the pressure of land and real estate speculators who would benefit from European Americans ready to sell their homes at market or below market rates. Of course, they feared that their homes would lose value as ethnic minorities moved into the neighborhood.

Not only was the community of Old Church changing, there were now the homeless and displaced at their doorsteps to think about. A skid row began to develop in the downtown neighborhood and the neighborhood property values began to plummet as the more unattractive members of society began to find a home in the downtown area. Businesses began to leave for more lucrative and physically attractive areas. A church that had always unconsciously worked hand-in-hand with community institutions was now being deserted as these institutions moved to supposedly greener pastures.

Soon the pressures of losing members to surrounding churches that had beat Old Church in obtaining prime upscale real estate on the outskirts of downtown, became too great for the leaders of Old Church. They had to decide whether to minister to their community or move to where the more affluent members of their congregation and city had headed. This was the first crisis of Old Church and the decision they made to move from their original location was a hard-fought battle as lines were drawn between the pastoral staff, lay leaders, and the membership. A consensus was impossible as the older leadership group was determined to try and reduplicate their success of twenty to thirty years ago in another location.

A Theological and Ethical Analysis of
an Old American Church

One pastor who was involved in the deliberations still cringed as he reminisced about the hard feelings generated by the various factions of the church. Physical violence was even threatened against the pastor by a few of the old leadership during some of the more heated moments and a number of his supporters who wanted to remain at the present site. It was this sense of intense conflict and soul searching that surrounded the momentous decision to seek greener pastures. I want to emphasize the conflictual nature of this move because I want you, the reader, to understand how issues of race and class are central to the church's identity in the United States of America.

When H. R. Niebuhr wrote his famous text, *Christ and Culture* in which he attempted to develop a topology of the Christian church's relationship to culture, he did not specifically mention these issues. Irrespective of this, it is a useful topology when one considers how central the role of culture is to the European American churches. In this work, Niebuhr divided the Christian Church into five different categories: 1) Christ against Culture; 2) Christ of Culture; 3) Christ above Culture; 4) Christ and Culture in Paradox; and 5) Christ the Transformer of Culture. Of Niebuhr's five types, three are of importance for our look at Old Church: Christ against Culture, Christ of Culture, and Christ Transformer of Culture. It is my belief that these three types are the most clearly defined and delineated categories. The Christ against Culture and Christ of Culture represent the extremes of rejection and acceptance of the culture by the churches and Christ the Transformer of Culture represents the ideal type of the church's relationship to culture.

Christ against Culture

The church representative of the Christ against Culture type is a church in which the church has taken an oppositional stance against the culture of its time. In Niebuhr's schema, this type is reflective of groups like monastic communities that have cut themselves off from the world and/or rejected the possibility of normal participation in the everyday life of the culture. They believe that the culture is entirely antithetical to the redemptive power of Christ and the church. They act accordingly by separating themselves from the social activities of their community. Niebuhr put forth monasticism as a form of this kind of theological and ethical position.

Christ of Culture

Just as the Christ against Culture stands at one end of Niebuhr's paradigm, the paradigm of Christ of Culture stands on the other extreme. This type of church is one that has adopted a stance that places itself in a non-conflicting relationship to its surroundings. In this paradigm, these churches have developed a philosophy in which the culture and the normative ideals of the Christian church are in agreement. The cultural expressions of a particular society are accepted as the status quo and are not opposed by the church. Instead, the church embraces the culture since the church believes that these cultural attitudes are similar to the values that exist in the church.

Niebuhr believes that nineteenth century Protestantism was reflective of this kind of paradigm. One may ask whether the churches of twentieth century Protestantism in general, and Old Church in particular, are most represented by this paradigm. It is interesting that it serves as an extreme type in Niebuhr's topology. I doubt whether most liberal Protestants would see themselves as extremists of any imaginable type of paradigm.

Old Church in Niebuhr's Paradigm

Niebuhr made the point that churches do not operate in a social vacuum. They are deeply embedded in particular cultural settings and these cultural settings may be viewed in various ways by the church. It is also important to realize that real churches are often composed of combinations of theological and ethical attitudes. They may exist simultaneously within the same person or group, or they may exist as opposing theological and ethical positions.

What I have described of American churches, and this church in particular, would place them in the category of churches that have developed an ethical and theological position that most resembles a church that reflects Christ of Culture. In this situation, the church takes an assimilationist view of their position regarding their cultural stance. This is not a church which rejects culture (Christ against Culture)—its supposed polar opposite—instead, it finds the cultural values and its own Christian values to be in agreement.

This is fine if the culture is indeed "Christian"—in the sense of a culture which promotes inclusivity and diversity. Modern social commentators, however, remind us of the failure of our society to fully integrate ethnic minorities and women into all levels of the social fabric. This means that this kind of church will be fine if it is in a situation where the culture remains stable. However, the story of American neighborhoods is one of continual cultural change. When this change occurs, these churches have little theological or ethical resources to respond to the changes in the culture around them. They may have assimilated into a European American middle-class culture, but when that culture is no longer the norm for that community, the church finds that its assimilationist nature is tied into a particular ethnic or class paradigm.

Christ the Transformer of Culture

Niebuhr also defines three other types that he identifies as mediating forms as opposed to the more extreme forms of Christ against Culture and Christ of Culture. These three are: Christ above Culture, which is represented by the Catholic tradition; Christ and Culture in Paradox, best represented by certain forms of Lutheranism; and Christ the Transformer of Culture, best represented by John Weiley and Augustine.

Niebuhr has been accused by some of advocating the Christ the Transformer paradigm. They claim that he moves beyond description of the church to a more proscriptive advocacy of this kind of church theology and ethics (see *The Christian Century*, June 19-26, 2002 pp.28-33). I am not bothered by this critique and, in fact, I believe that this is what Niebuhr intended despite his declarations of objectivity. As a postmodern advocate of the impossibility of scholarly neutrality, I find that Niebuhr's claim of objectivity is no longer necessary. It may have been necessary for someone who wrote about the church in the scholarly climate of his day and time.

Instead of needing to make a claim for objectivity, I celebrate the superiority of the Church as Transformer of Culture paradigm, and only wish that Niebuhr had made an even stronger case with a greater inclusion of the black churches that have historically committed to social and personal transformation. Black churches may have varied as to the level of their social activity but they have consistently preached the importance of social justice and individual holiness. They have not found it necessary to either stand apart or become captive to the culture. This, of course, is not without exception. Some forms of black Pentecostalism have stressed the separation of the culture from the church and some middle-class churches have not always faced their social obligations but, by and large, the theological and ethical stances of black churches would reinforce the normative goals of personal and social transformation of culture.

The metaphor of Pentecost best captures this ideal of the church as multicultural, interracial and class inclusive. It may be that the Christian church has yet to develop a paradigm that has been able to transform culture (Niebuhr's Christ the Transformer of Culture) in a meaningful way, despite its many attempts at transformation from Augustine to Calvin to Rausenbusch. Herein lies the bias. A church that does not critique a culture which promotes racism and classism cannot legitimately hold itself up as a model of Christian virtue.

In some ways, this book is a study of a church's struggle with pluralism as an expression of Christian ethics. It is easier to write books about pluralism than it is to write books on how to make it happen. Perhaps by examining the inner workings of a church caught in this dilemma, it will help others in similar situations to make better decisions. At least it will give those who favor a more pluralistic church the opportunity to understand some of the dynamics that will make its realization more than a notion.

Old Church and Crisis

Old Church made the decision to move from its downtown location and move up the hill to a more upscale neighborhood. It moved to a location that was midway between the old downtown location and the most prosperous residences in the hills. The location was in a beautiful setting with adequate parking and excellent educational and recreational space. The initial move of the church resulted in a spurt of growth. It seemed as though those who had fought for this change would, after all, be rewarded with a vibrant church.

The same problems, however, which Old Church ran from followed them to the new location. Urban sprawl soon caught up to their new location and they found themselves landlocked by housing and businesses that moved around their location. Persons of varying ethnic and class status began to move into their community. The clergy that served the church recognized the signs of their cultural isolation and continued their attempts to get the church to open up to its surrounding community. Efforts at outreach to the community through the development of food programs for the hungry and homeless and the opening up of the church to various community groups were attempts to demonstrate the church's openness to the community.

Unfortunately, these efforts did not result in any significant church growth. And, in fact, the decline proceeded in spite of the presence of new ministries and an open door policy. Members of the community who attended the church experienced the inhospitable attitudes of the leaders and its prominent members to accommodate and welcome them because of their different cultural and class backgrounds. It was not unusual for a hundred persons to visit the church during the year with only two or three deciding to join the church.

The older church leaders who still remained in the church had long ago formed a club that met monthly for fellowship and dinner. These persons constituted the inner circle of the church leadership. During their meetings, they would constantly remind themselves of the times when their children were present and the church was a thriving institution. However, they didn't ask themselves why their children and others from their children's generation no longer attended the church. There was a refusal to see how the culture around them had changed—not just racially and in terms of class—but even from a generational perspective. The Old Church leadership was out of step with the younger generation's desire for a spirituality that spoke to their needs and interests.

Soon the church reached a point of numerical no return and they were no longer able to provide the personnel to maintain the religious education program. The lack of a religious education program was detrimental to the church. New families visiting the church were not interested in returning since they sought congregations that could minister to the whole family— from the crib to the grave. The possibility of attracting new families and younger persons diminished as the church developed into a "siege complex."

New pastoral leadership often brought new hope but the new pastors soon found out that the old leadership of Old Church were a formidable group. They were not able to galvanize enough opposition from within the church, nor recruit enough members from outside the church to produce the desired cultural shift within the church. The Old Church members claimed that they wanted a healthy and vibrant church, however, they were not willing to cooperate with new leadership in their efforts to relinquish and redistribute the power.

The final crisis occurred when a particularly dynamic pastor attempted to lead the church to proclaim itself as a church that was open to gays, lesbians and transgendered persons. The efforts of the pastor, which included bringing in guest speakers to "speak objectively" about the subject, were vigorously opposed by the Old Church members. Even though one of the most prominent younger lay leaders in the church was a homosexual male and son of one of the church's oldest members, the church was unable to develop a civil way to discuss the issue. It became a lightning rod for persons who wanted the church to change, versus the Old Church leadership who wanted to return to the good old days.

This struggle resulted in the church voting to include in their church description, the affirmation of inclusiveness to gays. The vote ended in a tie with the minister casting the deciding vote. This led to a deeply split and resentful congregation. The Old Church leadership made things extremely uncomfortable for the new pastor. It resulted in the minister's early departure from her pastorate because of financial matters that the church's leadership would have otherwise been willing to authorize. It was a Pyrrhic victory for the pastor and her supporters as the church found itself once again racked by division and disagreement.

This incident in the life of this church made me realize how important leadership is in the life of the church. This particular pastor was extremely competent and in tune with the cultural diversity in the community. Her zeal, however, to create change resulted in further divisions in the church. In order for change to occur, it is necessary to pick one's battles wisely. And even though her politics were in line with the community's needs and attitudes, it was a battle. Had it been won, it would have had little effect on the composition of the church. The minister's decision to resign and remove herself from the church demonstrated to the Old Church members that they had the power to lead the church in the direction they chose.

The supporters of the pastor were concentrated in the Social Concerns Committee. This committee was headed by a relatively new, but mature couple who had been members of the church for several years. They were solid citizens in every way. The husband had been a very successful executive with one of the major corporations in the country. Additionally, they had moved to the community to live out their lives in a kind of semi-retirement and they gave a great deal of their time and money to the projects of the church.

Like most of the newer members, they were also more liberal politically and theologically than the Old Church members. Their daughter had adopted a child who was black and she also worked with urban teenagers who were involved in the juvenile justice system. The wife was the chair of the committee and was always looking for ways in which the church could expand its ministry to sectors of the community that had been overlooked. She and several others from the committee became involved in a long-term community organizing project that included persons and churches from ethnic minority groups and various social classes.

After the departure of the previous pastor, they continued to fight for gay inclusion in the church. They planned a worship service at which another committee member and one of the few younger church leaders was the featured speaker. He was one of the few openly gay persons in the congregation. The Social Concerns Committee was the only place where persons of different ethnicities or gender status were fully integrated in the church's fellowship.

This committee sought to continue its pro-gay stance as a matter of fact and in a non-confrontational manner. In addition to the worship service, they invited a local gay pastor to speak at their meeting, which led to the committee's participation in the community's Gay Pride March and Celebration. This was the first time that the church had publicly participated in the gay community's activities. They also sought ways that they could be helpful advocates for at-risk gay youth who were in the school system.

Participation at these meetings was never above five to seven persons. They would sometimes meet with members from the Missions Committee, which was responsible for more traditional church missional activities. For instance, the Mission

Committee sponsored the weekly dinners and shelter for homeless men, women and children. Once a week, homeless men would gather at the church for a meal that was prepared and served by various church members. After the meal, the men would be allowed to sleep in the recreational hall of the church.

This project was probably the most popular mission activity of the church. It soon, however, became apparent that the church was only scratching the surface of the problem and the chairperson and various members wondered aloud as to how the church could have a more direct and lasting impact on an increasingly serious homeless situation in the community. The tremendous increases in rental prices, along with a rental shortage, had created hundreds of homeless families and the community was searching for an adequate and equitable way to provide for this population.

In other writings, I have described a term called "the ministry circle." This is a phrase that has to do with a church's ability to minister with the objects of its mission activity. Instead of developing ministries with persons in the community who are in need, the church has a tendency to do charity work in which community members receive aid but they are never invited or challenged to lead the ministry effort. This leads to a form of paternalism that is eventually disempowering for the church and the ministry.

This ministry style often hides deep-seeded patterns of institutional racism or classism. An example of this ministry style can be seen in a church program I was hired to develop and supervise for a large Midwestern church. The church was in a neighborhood that was experiencing racial change. European Americans had begun to leave the neighborhood in increasing numbers and the housing was beginning to deteriorate. The neighborhood quickly became populated by single parent households whose members were under-employed and under-educated. In an attempt to respond to the needs of the community, the church developed a summer program with money from their denominational headquarters. I was hired to work with the church as they were in the process of developing their ministry efforts.

The pastor of the church was very sensitive to the situation of the community. I encouraged him and accompanied him on visits to the households in the immediate neighborhood. We soon discovered the presence of several crack houses that were close to the church and gained a general feel for the social problems facing this community. I will never forget how the pastor insisted that, even though he wanted to help the persons in the community, he was not a social worker. I found it strange that he would separate the church's social ministry from its spiritual ministry. He, however, was particularly sensitive to charges and accusations from fellow pastors in less socially-challenging situations that his church was engaging in social work as opposed to Christian ministry.

I lived with one of the church families. I, therefore, got to know several of the church families quite well. I found that the leaders of the church's youth ministry had a difficult time in getting close to the young African American participants in the program. The children also realized this sense of social distance. One day, one of the boys refused to take his plate to the counter after the meal. When I asked him to comply with the rules, he replied that I didn't even know his name. Of course, I did know his name and after calling him by his name, I insisted that he take his plate to the counter. He smiled sheepishly and complied.

During the next staff meeting, I asked the church members about their relationship with the African American children and insisted that they take the effort to become more personally involved with them. I also explained that the youth who I described above was in need of that kind of personal contact. I had learned that this child's mother had been arrested for possession of crack cocaine. He was in a bad mood because of the implications of her arrest and possible incarceration. I found it illuminating that the youth of the church were aware of the attitudes of their parents. I was invited to dinner at the home of a church member whose several teenagers worked as counselors in the summer program. After dinner, the youth told me that their parents were afraid of the ten-year-old black boys who were coming to the church's program. When I expressed my disbelief, they reminded me of the various incidents that had occurred during the summer when the older members of the church showed fear or acted inappropriately. The young persons knew that their parents were involved in the programs out of a sense of guilt and obligation but could not hide their true feelings of fear. I later spoke to the pastor about this situation and he admitted that it was true and that if the church members could not overcome their fear of the African Americans in their community, then the church would eventually go the way of other churches in their area and move out of the community or die.

This was also the situation in Old Church. Often members of Old Church found themselves ministering *to* and not *with* the community, while at the same time, numerous community groups served the community by using the space provided by Old Church. What the church lacked was a staff and membership to fully implement their mission and ministry goals. The church, however, showed little desire in really getting to know the persons in need who came to the church. This is something that the church consultant attempted to address. I will speak about this and other features of Old Church in this their time of crisis.

CHAPTER 3

The Challenge of Church A

■■

W HILE I WAS AT OLD CHURCH, I decided that I wanted to be active in the life of the church. I decided to join and see if I could be of some service. I decided that I wanted to get in touch with my earlier days as a layperson and deacon. I was also a former Youth and Young Adult Director as well as former campus minister. Little did I know I would soon be a participant/observer for the purposes of writing a book that I hoped would help me and others to understand the factors that lead to church decline.

The pastor welcomed my attendance and participation and soon asked me if I wanted to serve as a kind of honorary minister of community relations. I accepted this unpaid volunteer position and began to learn more about the church and its ministry to the community. My main role was to meet with the Social Concerns Committee, a small group of laypersons, who sought to develop social ministries for the church.

At this time, Old Church had an average attendance of approximately fifty persons. The Sunday School no longer existed because there were not enough children or volunteers to teach Sunday School classes. The average age of church members was well over fifty with many of the leaders having retired or at least, semi-retired. There was a smattering of young persons who were children of some of the older members but they were a distinct minority. Old Church was primarily an aging European American congregation. Its interim minister was an older pastor who had been appointed to the church in an effort to heal some of the wounds left over from the previous pastor's service.

In October of that year, the church hired a consultant to help them develop a plan that would save their church from extinction. The consultant was a retired pastor who had much success in developing churches in that part of the country. He had grown up in that area and was familiar with the concerns of the community. He had also been asked to preach at that church several times and was, therefore, familiar with that church and its leadership. He had been successful as a pastor during the booming times when the community was growing along with the church. This pastor was practically raised in the same community as Old Church and had been a successful pastor not more than twenty miles from the site of Old Church. Now, as an elder pastor, he was expected to give guidance to struggling congregations. He had taken the requisite courses in church growth and leadership so he had the academic as well as the practical experience to lead this kind of consultation.

In other words, he had all the necessary requirements to help Old Church. No one could claim that he was not an experienced pastor or that he did not have a feel for the congregation and its problems. He was the perfect consultant for a church in its peculiar situation.

The consultant first met with a representative number of persons in the church in order to gain a sense of the strengths and weaknesses, and the desires and hopes of the church leadership. He reported the results and recommendations of his study at a Saturday meeting of the church.

Consultant's Report

The consultant developed a detailed, twelve-page report regarding the church's condition and his recommendations. It primarily dealt with the strengths of the church. In fact, if one didn't know better it would have been difficult to tell that the church was in a state of extreme crisis. In reality, it was only able to pay its bills because it had rented out much of its educational space to a private school which brought in enough income to pay most of the church's operating expenses. The church would have faced a financial crisis that would have led to a more immediate sense of its problems without this income.

The tone of the report was extremely upbeat. The consultant detailed why the present members of the church continued to attend and what they saw as the important features of the church. According to the consultant, out of a list that included Challenge, Tradition and Reason, the church's most important features were Compassion and Good Times/Fellowship. These categories were taken from a list developed by noted church consultant, Kennon Callahan.

The church, as the consultant noted, had indeed developed a reputation for being a place which was known for its compassion for the socially marginal. The church allowed its buildings to be used by various community organizations that were ministering to persons who were homeless, addicted, or suffering from various social and personal ills. The congregation rarely participated in these ministries but at least they were open to having their facilities used by these organizations. They, therefore, saw themselves as compassionate and open to healing the hurts of their community.

They had also developed an active social life among themselves. Various Old Church members had developed a quasi religious/social group called the Sunshine Group that met once monthly. During these meetings they shared a common meal and usually had some type of religious devotion. This group represented the membership that had been at the church for decades before the present move to its newest location. The men in this group were the most reluctant to welcome change and often opposed the previous pastors in their attempts to change the direction of the church. This group will henceforth be known as Old Guard.

Another group composed of long-time members was a women's group dedicated to missionary work. This women's group was also a close knit group of the wives and friends of the Old Guard. It also gave the church a sense of compassion for the less fortunate by discussing the social needs of the community as well as broader social issues as identified in their denominational literature.

Both of these groups had a discretely-defined membership that only valued its present members. They were reluctant to open themselves to new members and persons outside of the church who may have otherwise been a part of the fellowship of the church. They valued their companionship and developed a false sense of mission at the same time. As I was to examine the reasons why the church continued to decline, I would see how lacking they were in Challenge, Tradition and Reason.

The consultant also made a list of items needing special attention. These included developing more small groups that would increase their sense of fellowship, developing an action plan for the church's growth and improving the lighting and sound system in the sanctuary. These problems don't appear to be too severe, but for a church that was on the brink of extinction, each item gained special importance.

The consultant also felt the church should be willing to inventory its assets so that it could support the changes that were necessary for its survival. This included increasing the church staff to employ a Christian Education person and expanding the music ministry. He also recommended that the church should develop women's and men's retreats and groups that would emphasize spirituality and leadership. It was also recommended that the worship time be moved from eleven to ten o'clock on Sunday moving with an eleven-thirty Bible study hour.

When the consultant was pushed for his prediction concerning the survival of the church if his recommendations were not implemented, he stated that he gave the church six months—at best—to survive if no positive changes were implemented. This stark prediction made his recommendations much more immediate and necessary, yet I didn't sense a feeling of urgency among the members who were present during his presentation. The consultant also noted that the church had at least a million dollars worth of property that could be liquidated and used for the redevelopment of the church. In this sense, the church membership was fortunate to be in a situation where it had the financial resources to rekindle the life of the church.

Whether the church lived or died did not depend on the lack of financial resources. It depended on the will of the church and its ability to see beyond its present situation. It was not a question of resources but of a willingness to develop a church that was open to its community. I felt the consultant was soft with the membership on this issue. In speaking to him, however, he believed that it was better to work in a positive manner rather than develop resistance by identifying how the membership had developed a closed stance toward the community. I was anxious to see how others in the church viewed the consultant's recommendations and what it would mean for the possibility of life or death for this congregation. I was convinced that their decision to live or die would hinge on their willingness to make urgent and immediate changes.

The consultant's depiction of the church as a church which valued Compassion and Fellowship places it in the theological and ethical Christ of Culture category. The church took some pride in being reflective of the normative values of the community. Those ideals of a close family, respectable businesses, the achievement of the American Dream of home ownership, and political centrism were the values most expressed by the church members who were a part of the Old Church. This perspective was often challenged by newer members to the church and by some of the pastors of the church.

The church consultant did not really address how the church was divided along theological and ethical lines or how the church would be able to overcome these differences in its attempt to develop a healthy and vibrant congregation. These divisions in the church became more and more apparent during my stay and as the church leaders prepared to deal with the implications of the consultant's report. In order for change to occur, there has to be sufficient motivation. One would think that the prospect of the church's closure would have provided enough impetus for the church leadership to make immediate decisions. They should have been able to agree with the consultant's suggestions that would at least place the church on firm financial and programmatic ground. I fully expected the church's leadership to adopt the suggestions of the consultant and I would witness a church that had been on the brink of death come back to life. What happened subsequent to that meeting was a surprise and is subject to much interpretation.

Reaction to the Church Consultant

After a month, it became apparent that the church's leadership did not share the consultant's sense of urgency regarding its need to make immediate and significant structural changes. Although the leaders met to intentionally discuss and implement the consultant's recommendations, only those recommendations that required the least amount of change were implemented and those occurred only gradually and with little energy or urgency.

The church leadership, including its current pastor, developed a strategy of denial to deal with the consultant's bad news. Their denial did not take the form of a detailed or thorough discussion of the issues or recommendations. Instead, the denial took the form of anti-intellectualism and skepticism concerning the consultation process. In fact, the greatest strength of the consultant—the fact that he knew the community and was personally familiar with its history—was turned against him. In this case, familiarity bred contempt as the church leadership treated him more like a friend than a respected church official. One of the ironies of this particular situation was that the consultant had been a member of my ordination board some twenty years before, a connection that proved valuable as I discussed with him the church's response to his recommendations.

It was interesting to me how the church adopted a general business culture approach to the role of the church consultant. Many of them had climbed the corporate ladder and had extensive experience with consultants. They began to uniformly make jokes about consultants as persons who could give advice but who did not have to live with the consequences. They had many stories of consultants in their business dealings who were little more than nuisances. I was especially surprised by their reaction, since most of the leadership had known the consultant over a period of anywhere from five to thirty years. He was often asked by them to speak at various occasions and meetings long before his retirement and new role as a consultant.

I took their reactions to be reflective of an unwillingness to change the general direction of the church rather than a serious critique of consultancy. Even the pastor, who often spoke of the consultant with great respect, was extremely skeptical of his recommendations. He saw them as being unrealistic and not necessary for immediate implementation. The pastor and the consultant were very friendly and shared many common experiences but when it came to taking his recommendations seriously, this was not on the pastor's radar.

As the weeks turned into months and the church's membership began to further decline, I was asked by one of the church leaders about the prospects of the church. I told him that I agreed with the consultant and that unless the church was willing to make drastic changes, at the end of the six-month period, they would have little choice but to prepare for their demise. I asked him about the state of the church leadership's plans to act on the recommendation of the consultant. He defended the church leadership's plans to eventually implement the consultant's recommendation but that it would take time to do the things that were necessary. I replied that from my perspective and from the statements from the consultant, this gradualist approach that denied the extent of the church's crisis situation would not be enough to keep the church alive.

This lack of urgency from the leadership was also reflective of and reinforced by the current pastor of the church. The pastor often felt himself at the mercy of the Old Guard. He often expressed a fear of as well as an admiration for this group. He felt financially dependent on this group since they were the primary benefactors of the church. He often expressed a concern that a particular church member had decided to stop giving since the pastor had said something that did not meet that particular person's expectations.

This fear of financial dependency was often substituted by a kind of admiration for that segment of the church. Despite the grim outlook of the church's prospects, he would often state that the church was a great church and that it should not be criticized too heavily. The pastor's lack of courage to take on the Old Church's stranglehold of the church's life and his flights of fancy regarding the church's future meant that the consultant's picture of a dying church was not being taken seriously by any of the church's leadership.

One of my duties was to attend the church's Social Concerns committee. As the six-month deadline approached, I was asked by the group what I thought the church's problems were and how this could be changed. I basically stated what I have been addressing in these pages: that the church was out of step culturally and the church's leadership was not moving quickly enough to make the necessary changes for the church to overcome its problems. The pastor took great pains to disagree with my assessment and once again emphasized the greatness of the church.

After the meeting, others in the committee expressed surprise at the vehemence that the pastor brought to his defense of the church, especially since we had spent the last four months as a committee speaking about the problems in the church. Since the committee was composed of persons who were a part of the smaller leadership group that was new to the church, they were hard put to understand the pastor's position. Because of my position as a ministerial colleague, I could not be as critical as I wanted to be in this situation. It was enough that they saw the differences in our position.

Regardless, even though we discussed the cultural issues it was difficult for this group to see itself leading the church in a positive direction. They had expended whatever social capital they had in the fight for a sexually-inclusive church and even though they were painfully aware of how European American and middle-class their church was, they saw little hope of changing the focus of the church. They saw themselves as a more socially progressive leadership in that they were willing to minister to the social outcasts of the community. They had sponsored a visit from a pastor who had taken a national stance for the inclusion of gays in the church. They had also been involved in a program that involved feeding the homeless.

One of my criticisms of their efforts was the social distance that still existed in their efforts. They may have been willing to take a stance for gays and the homeless, but the gay and homeless population still did not feel welcome to attend the church and they had done little to encourage these persons to become a part of the church's fellowship. Once again, the consultant's view of the church as one of Compassion and Fellowship was true but the compassion for others did not lead to an inclusion of the objects of their compassion in the life of the church.

Latent Meanings

As I mentioned previously, I felt as though the skepticism and denial of the church consultant's recommendations was a surface response that was not indicative of the true depth of the church's theological orientation that was preventing them from making the necessary changes. Both the church's Old Guard and new leadership were captives of their respective cultural orientation. Whether this cultural orientation represented a more conservative or liberal culture it was still a position in which the culture and the church were in consort with each other. The respective groups could critique each other's cultural stance but they were both mired in their own cultural perspective with little room for a theological or ethical critique that could lead them to a rebirth and transformation.

Niebuhr's categories should not be mistaken to mean that the Christ of Culture orientation is somehow conservative and the Christ the Transformer of Culture position is more liberal. I believe that this church's multiple cultural orientations disguised a theological and ethical orientation that made this church unable to deal with cultural diversity regardless of whether the stance was conservative or liberal. I found the new leadership had a difficult time of understanding this perspective. I believe that they thought that since I was a black person I would be more sympathetic to their attempts at liberal reformism.

One of my ministry efforts at the church involved a series of lectures and presentations on the life and thoughts of the Rev. Dr. Martin Luther King Jr. For four Sundays after the morning worship service, I led the church in a discussion of several of King's sermons and I showed videotapes of the Civil Rights Movement. This event spoke volumes about the problems and possibilities this church had in developing an intercultural, interclass ministry.

Soon after the Social Concerns committee agreed that I should conduct this workshop there was a sudden vacuum of leadership. The pastor who had been excited about the class suddenly began to withdraw from the plans for the class, leaving the members of the committee in limbo as to what or who was in charge of planning and carrying out the workshop. We finally had a meeting and the new leadership group and I took control of planning the class. I believe that the pastor may have been afraid of the reaction of the more conservative group and unconsciously became more distant from the process. To the committee's credit, several of the new leadership group stepped forward and the workshop proceeded.

It turned out to be a powerful spiritual experience for all involved, including the pastor. After four weeks of discussion and prayer about the depth of King's spiritual commitment to his role as a Civil Rights leader, there were many powerful moments of prayer and fellowship as we discussed the depths of our own commitments to our own spiritual and social concerns. Yet even in this context it was difficult for the church's leadership to examine the social position of the church and its need for a theological reorientation.

I came to appreciate the members of the church as they struggled with King's commitment, but at the same time, I was intrigued by their inability to face the very situation that King was addressing in his sermons. It may be that most churches in this situation do not have the psychological resilience to examine this potentially painful situation. I found it interesting that I would receive little notes or gifts from persons who were not in the center of the church's leadership. Those persons who were on the margins due to class, age or ethnicity would speak to me with appreciation for the class, but it would be done on the margins of the class time. It was almost as though I recognized their marginality and it was a painful place for them to be because they wanted to be a fuller part of the church's ministry.

Six Months Later

Approximately six months after the church consultant made his recommendations, the members of the church were invited by an area church official to attend a meeting where they and two other churches, who were of similar size, would come together to discuss their situations. There was much rumor and innuendo that accompanied this meeting and many of the congregants felt as though the denomination had already made a decision as to the viability of Old Church. Since the time of the first consultation the denomination had brought in a church architect who assessed the value of the property and gave the church recommendations regarding their facilities. The architect was not sympathetic to the church remaining in its present location. Like many, he noted how unattractive the sanctuary was to the average churchgoer. It was very dark inside and it was often difficult to even read the church bulletin and hymnal during the service.

Once again, the church leadership did not feel particularly motivated by the architect's opinion and blithely went on as usual. One step that the pastor had made was to create a ministry team out of himself, myself and the Minister of Music. Instead of expanding her role as the Minister of Music as recommended by the consultant, the pastor decided that all the church could afford to do was make more efficient use of her time. She attempted to develop a fuller ministry that would have included children in the community but without the church's financial and spiritual support she soon became discouraged and left the church, although she claimed other more personal reasons for leaving.

It was plain to me that if the church had asked her to become a full-time staff person with the church and paid her accordingly, that she would have gladly developed a dynamic music ministry for the church. Instead, she was left to her own devices to try and develop a community music program that would be based at the church but not a fully integrated ministry effort of the church. Once again the church leadership could not support an effort that would have involved a more diverse community within the church.

Several of the men of the church also began a quiet attempt at a Men's Fellowship. This was created by men from the Old Guard and new leadership for the stated purpose of increasing the opportunity for the men of the church to get to know one another. However, there was no agenda stated and it was emphasized that there was not to be an agenda. I felt as though this was an attempt to come together without dealing with any of the issues that separated them and which plagued the church. The meetings never had more than five men and, once again, showed a pattern of good intention but fear at efforts involving transformation.

The other recommendations made by the consultant went unheeded. The most important one involved liquidating some of the church's assets to expand the church's ministry. The leadership claimed that there was too much red tape to effectively develop this recommendation. It was also apparent that the church leadership was afraid that any attempt to sell property would result in resistance by Old Church members and so, even though certain steps were taken in preparation for selling some of the property, concrete steps to sell or even borrow against the property were avoided.

Crossroads—Reality Sets In

The three churches were called to a Saturday meeting where the fate of their churches would be discussed. The meeting with the three churches was the first time I saw the Old Guard and new leadership realize the desperate position that the church was in. Even though they knew intellectually that the church could not continue as a viable entity, with its continually flagging attendance and lack of spirit, the church members never let the possibility of the loss become an emotional reality.

The area church official came prepared to fully inform the churches of their situation. She also brought consultants from the denominational offices who interpreted the churches' financial and social situations. They brought demographic information regarding the area that the churches were located in so that the members could see that there was a great potential for growth and life. They also were clear that each of the churches was in a severe crisis and that the only viable alternative was going to involve some combination of the death or merger of one or two of the congregations.

Their recommendations hit the church like a ton of bricks. They could no longer live in a fantasy or luxury of playing at church. The area church official made it plain that she wanted them to begin meeting with the idea of the recombination of the church's resources. The next Sunday the pastor called a special meeting after church to discuss the situation with the general membership. This was the beginning of the church leadership's recognition that they had come to a point of no return and that they simply did not have the energy, vision or leadership to turn around the fate of the church. There would be no miracle revival of Old Church. A part or all of it was about to die.

The church leadership was now certain that there was no way that Old Church was going to survive in its present form. Their attempts at denial did not change the facts of their situation and they had to come to grips with this very unpleasant reality. They also had to lead the church in the realization that change was inevitable and that their fate was no longer in their hands. Old Church was not going to continue to exist in a limited fashion and slowly die on the vine. Nor was it going to make a miracle recovery and become what it once had been. Times had changed and the church hadn't, and according to its church polity, its area church officials had the right to call for the church to reorganize instead of allowing it to continue in its diminished state.

Some churches that have a more independent polity, where the church was responsible for its own governance without being responsible to higher church structures, like most Baptist and Congregational churches, have often been satisfied to allow the church to exist for years in its diminished state. In this state, with very little ministry or other activity coming forth from the church, the church becomes a church in word and not deed.

It is the opinion offered here that this is not life but a kind of comatose state where the church is analogous to a terminal patient on life support.

A telling statement made by the area official which brought the crisis situation into plain view to the church leadership was that Old Church's present status would not even meet the requirements of a new church start. A congregation at the paltry level of membership, giving and ministry of Old Church and its two sister churches respectively would not have met the requirements for church membership in its denomination. They would have been seen as missionary churches that needed a helping hand from the denomination. The only practical hope for these churches was that they should combine and develop a new ministry that would meet the needs of their community. Alone, they would continue to limp along and the denomination would not continue to subsidize failing churches. Their only hope at life would be the result of a shedding of their old identities and the forging of something new.

New Start

In response to the crisis, each of the three area churches was asked to form a committee that would meet in order to plan for the coming change in church configuration. Old Church found itself in a process that it hoped to avoid, but now that it was inevitable that change would occur, they wanted to be an important factor in that process. Old Church was willing to accept the inevitable and did not attempt to oppose the process. They used humor, leading to a kind of gallows humor, to disguise the pain they were experiencing. It was obvious that they were disappointed but they also realized that in some way they were responsible for the church's situation.

They had refused to mentor a younger or more diverse leadership in the church and on several occasions they had often threatened to withhold finances if their will was not accepted on various church matters. It was not uncommon that many of the new leadership group, or even those who were members of the church who were not in leadership positions, would often comment on the near dictatorial attitudes of the Old Church faction.

Conflicts often arose over issues of building use. Even though the church had become open to many community groups, there was a lot of tension over the care and maintenance of the building. Rules regarding building use were strictly enforced and members who were involved in ministry efforts were vigilant in making sure that they did not give the Old Church members any reason to oppose their use of the building. The decision to close the church was the inevitable result of years of "us against them" thinking that extended to the new church site.

This proprietary sense over the church facilities was a major reason why I didn't think the church would be open to the recommendations of the first church consultant. The church had acquired several important art pieces that were displayed prominently throughout the church. One of the recommendations by the consultant was that these art pieces should be sold in order to fund the mission of the church. The consultant emphasized that the church was lucky to have these kinds of assets since so many churches in their situation are forced to close their doors because of the lack of financial means.

This recommendation brought an immediate negative reaction. It was apparent that these were more than artifacts used to spruce up or decorate the church. The artifacts had achieved symbolic value and represented for the Old Church their earlier days of glory and prominence. Any action that challenged the Old Church's sense of church identity was met with a kind of quiet resistance. They were incapable of envisioning a church that was independent of the church's past. Those members who were new to the church did not have the same vested interest in preserving those church properties. They had no symbolic value for the new leadership or new members. The church was now operating out of conflicting symbol systems.

This meant that it would be very difficult for this church to move as quickly as was necessary to achieve their goal of a revitalized ministry. Six months was not long enough to allow the church to grieve the loss of its old place in the community. The previous pastor had become embroiled in her political agenda to guide the church in this process of loss, mourning and recovery. The present pastor was too much of a "people pleaser" to lead the church in making unpleasant decisions. In fact, he was in a state of grieving over the break-up of his marriage and he had little energy to offer to a church that was in a crisis of its own.

The Old Guard's failure to come to grips with the loss of its previous status was evident in a class I was asked to lead. The class was composed of mainly Old Guard women who were studying the mission of the church. This particular lesson was on the mission of the church to urban areas and I was asked to lead the class. After explaining the process of urbanization in the United States and the possible responses by the church I was genuinely surprised by the responses and questions of the class. I discovered that most of them were raised in extremely rural areas. Their primary geographic identity was not urban or suburban but rural. They took most of their values and religious perspective from the rural church setting.

I was surprised by their orientation and felt as though I was in another time and space with persons who had little love or appreciation for the urban world in which they lived. It helped me to understand why their children, who grew up in a thoroughly urban world, had not found a place in the church. The Old Guard leadership had not changed its core values to reflect the issues of modern urban families. They had come to age and been successful in a world that did not challenge their rural, small-town values. Their memories were not the memories of urban Americans. Their language was not the language of urban America. All those sociological and theological categories like memory, language, politics, etc. were of a different stripe than their urban community with its diversity of class, race and gender.

This was a painful understanding for the members of the class as they recognized how different their values were from those whom they were trying to reach. They also realized how different they were from their own children and to some extent how different they were from the pastors who had attempted to lead them to minister to their urban setting. The present pastor was much more like them in terms of his sociological markers. He, too, had grown up during the same time period and shared many of their values. This was probably why he often expressed an uncritical acceptance of their attitudes and behaviors. His empathy was an important reason why he had been chosen to lead the church, but he was often unable to use his skills as a trained counselor to help them move to an acceptance of their crisis. Those persons who were new leadership were very open to this process and hoped that it would result in a revitalized ministry to the community.

The other churches were in similar positions as Old Church and one of the churches in particular was very similar to Old

Church. Unlike Old Church, they stayed in their urban location and were deeply involved in the community's social needs. They, too, were faced with a dwindling older congregation and were very proud of their record of service to the community. Like Old Church they could not gain a critical distance from their situation in order to see that no matter how socially progressive and liberal they were, they were still unable to welcome diversity into their church.

At one of the planning meetings over fifteen persons were in attendance. When one of the leaders at Old Church mentioned that the churches were out of step culturally there was immediate resistance from the group. They refused to discuss the situation of their churches in relation to how they were aligned or misaligned with the cultural situation that surrounded them. Instead, each church attempted to assert its uniqueness and strengths. One of the churches was involved in a church growth ministry that was structured along the lines of a homogenous cultural model that was geared to attract similar persons of race and class. The other church was much like Old Church but emphasized a social ministry that was more incorporated into the life of the church.

Sociology of Religion—Gustafson's Model

It might be helpful at this stage to try and summarize the situation of these churches by using a sociological model first developed by James Gustafson in *Treasures in Earthen Vessels*. In this text Gustafson attempted to develop a model of analysis that took into account the church as a social institution. He examined various facets of the church as models of human communities, albeit with a theological foundation that also distinguished its purpose and functioning. The church's social structures were viewed from the viewpoint of the church as a human community, a natural community, a political community and as communities of language, memory and understanding, and belief and action.

The job of the three churches was to try and develop a community that was coherent, out of three similar but still distinct communities. As I have mentioned, two of the churches were much more similar in these areas and many persons thought that it would be better if only these two churches merged. Instead, the decision was made that all three churches would join in the merger process, thereby making a difficult task even more strenuous. Perhaps the greatest differences between the two similar churches and the third church was their views concerning the role of the church as a community of interpreters and as a political community.

The church with a homogenous growth program was also more conservative in its attitude toward the Bible. The pastor was much more conservative in his approach to the scriptures than the other two churches, and pastors who were engaged in biblical interpretation that was more influenced by liberation theologians or popular spirituality movements. I predict that this will be a continuing problem in the merger strategy of the churches. Many of the members attending the two more aligned churches were very articulate in why they were comfortable with their church's particular approach to the Scripture. Several of them chose those churches because they were not in the fundamentalist biblical camp.

Even though all three churches were involved in and approved of social ministries to the community, the more conservative biblical church saw its outreach as a direct extension of its desire to increase its membership as a biblically-based church. The other churches were not as concerned with using their social ministries to build their church attendance and membership. At one of the merger meetings, one of the members stated that he had no interest in saving the souls of anyone; his primary interest was in the church's role in easing human suffering.

Once again, it will be very difficult to merge churches who have such a distinctive difference in biblical and political understandings of their roles and missions. It might be helpful for churches to have a way of assessing where they stand in relation to their cultural surrounding. I believe that this can best be done by assessing their church according to Neibuhr's five categories and even more so by using Gustafson's sociological description for a more in-depth description of their church. I have analyzed the ministry of several churches, from mega-churches to small neighborhood churches who have developed successful ministries to their community. By using Gustafson's categories as an understanding of the church as a human community I hope to show how churches can assess themselves and develop an agenda for a transformative ministry.

CHAPTER 4

Living Churches

■■

Church #1— New Life

I WILL FIRST DESCRIBE A CHURCH that underwent a positive transformation that was of roughly the same size and condition of that of Old Church. Like Old Church it was faced with its imminent death before the church received a new pastor who was committed to a ministry that was multicultural and socially transformative. Like most churches it was not just a church that could be characterized as a Transformer of Culture type. It had elements of Christ against and of Culture in its theological and ethical style. However, it came to grips with its existence as a European American church in imminent danger of losing its ability to minister in and to a community that no longer reflected its social and economic characteristics. Thirty years ago it was a typical European American church with a Christ of Culture perspective. Indeed, the pastor told me that it took pride in being the last institution of its type in the community and therefore saw itself as a kind of last stand for the typical European American church.

The neighborhood itself had gone through several demographic changes in the past thirty years. It had once been an almost rural area on the edge of a medium-sized city. It soon grew to be a thriving middle-class suburb that was dominated by government workers who worked out of a facility that had been built in that community. However, after about twenty years of relative stability as an ideal suburban European American middle-class community, European American flight began to occur and most of the members moved farther out into the suburban terrain. Presently, the neighborhood is predominantly African American although there are several families and local business institutions, like a deli and barber shop, that continued in the neighborhood. These persons stayed because either they could not afford to move or because they genuinely enjoyed living in this part of their city.

The pastor reported that membership went from over 400, with an average worship attendance of more than 150 per Sunday, to a total church enrollment of sixty persons over this time span. The church was led by three older women who ranged in age from sixty-five to eighty-three years of age. These women basically ran most aspects of the church from the church board to the church choir. There were two African Americans in the church, the church was without a Sunday School, regular Bible study or youth ministry. When the new pastor arrived, he had as his goal to lead the church into being reflective of and responsive to its community. That meant that the church would have to become multicultural. One of this pastor's advantages was that he modeled his theological convictions in his own life. He was married to an Asian woman and was the father of two biracial children. He believed that it was possible to turn the church around or else he was certain that it would die of its own shortcomings as more and more of the church members became too aged to participate or just passed away.

He realized that the church was open to African Americans as a place of ministry but not as a place where African Americans were invited to be a part of the church. The church had sponsored a Narcotics Anonymous group that had been meeting at the church for several years. The pastor began to attend those meetings and he found many spiritually-grounded persons who had overcome their addictions through their belief in a Higher Power within the context of the small group movement that marked many self help groups. He began to invite those persons in the NA meetings to attend the church's services and he especially welcomed those whom he felt had leadership abilities to consider whether this church could be a place where they could exercise those abilities in the service of the church.

One of the leaders of the NA group, a middle-aged black man, accepted his invitation and became a part of the church council. The pastor described this leader as someone who refused to be ignored by the older European American members of the church. He went out of his way to introduce himself to all the members of the church and to get to know them through face-to-face encounters on a weekly basis. When he realized that he was being shunned by a particular member, he would go out of his way to confront the person with his presence in a non-threatening manner. As the black church membership began to slowly increase, the pastor lead the church council to sponsor a dialogue on race relations. This dialogue was facilitated by another black community member who later became a part of the leadership team of the church.

Although the pastor reported that the black and European American members spent most of the time talking past each other and becoming frustrated at their different positions, this encounter allowed the two groups to begin to listen to each other and form the basis for further growth. One church official who was at one of their board meetings, that by the end of the pastor's second year had become thoroughly integrated, remarked that it was obvious that there were two groups in the church defined by ethnicity that could not communicate to each other with any degree of cohesion. However, after the third year, many barriers had broken down and the pastor reported that this obvious racial divide was no longer a prominent factor in the church's life.

When I asked how this occurred, he stated that he thought it was due to the decision by the black members of the church to develop a choir that was more devoted to gospel music in its traditional and contemporary forms. He stated that soon after this choir was formed, many European Americans also joined the choir and it became a favorite time in the life of the church. So much so that even many of the older European American members began to rearrange their schedules so that they wouldn't miss the choir's performance.

The church slowly became more diverse as other neighborhood persons began to attend the church. He mentioned one European American woman in particular who was the mother of two biracial children who became very active in the leadership of the church. In addition to the choir, the church leadership began to develop small groups, including a men's group, and youth group that was thoroughly integrated. The time that I visited the church I noted the integrated choir practice and the easy way in which the older European American members were interacting with the new members. It was obvious that a real transformation had taken place.

The pastor emphasized that it was necessary to meet on a regular basis with new members. Part of this was accomplished through Bible study and council meetings. The church also became more active in the community and began to develop relationships with the schools and other local institutions. One such partnership resulted in a spring neighborhood festival that was coordinated by the church that resulted in the neighborhood regaining a lost sense of pride. The church also sponsored family dances where youth and families could enjoy fellowship under the sponsorship of the church. At the time of the pastor's call to another church, the church began to become active with other churches in an organization that was geared toward assessing neighborhood issues and developing strategies for social change.

They also sponsored a forum centered on issues of mult-culturalism at which more than 175 persons from around the city attended. The church had moved from being a group of elderly European American church persons, who were primarily interested in holding on to what was left of its past, to a thriving multicultural church that was now reaching out to its community. It had not neglected to minister to the spiritual needs of its members as witnessed by its ministry of music and Bible studies, but it also now found room to be a church that was as concerned about social transformation by including those who had been the social outcasts of their city. This was a far cry from the church that three years earlier was on the brink of a slow, European American death.

Analysis—The Church as Human Community

This church gives evidence of recovery from its imminent death through a process of group development that is much like the movement from childhood to adulthood. It goes through a process of growth after a protracted period of reflection and learning that is led by the pastor and the future leaders of the church. There is a kind of initiation process at work, similar to the process of initiation that occurs among people who have formal rites and training processes where boys are taught to become men, and girls women. Like the social process of Bar/Bat Mitzvah in the Jewish faith, these church leaders learn what it means to be responsible for the life of the corporate body.

As we just saw, the pastor began to initiate persons who used the church for their own spiritual needs, in this case Narcotics Anonymous. The pastor develops a level of trust between himself and the participants of the NA group by becoming a part of their meetings and eventually offering them the opportunity to exercise leadership in the church. This is a process that is accomplished through continual face-to-face interaction where conversation and Bible study become the focal points of the initiation process.

It is not the conversation or the Bible study that are the most important dynamics. Instead, they are the vehicles for the transformation process. It is not an easy task to take persons from a different and marginalized ethnic group, who were formerly addicted to narcotics, to places of leadership in an all European American religious setting. The pastor becomes the leader, or better yet, bridge, for this process. As far as he is able to identify with both groups he can provide a means of constructing a place for this new leadership group. By providing spaces for the two groups to explore their particular identities he can initiate a process of transformation that will eventually extend to the entire church. Their previous identity as a European American church will be challenged and transformed to a church that is diverse, inclusive and multicultural.

The language of this new identity is grounded in the pastor's, and eventually the members', biblical interpretation. They find in the New Testament a language of inclusiveness that grounds their efforts at transformation. The pastor's sermons, and examples of reaching across racial lines in his own personal life become teaching tools for the church. The pastor is aware that not all biblical language is inclusive and he is conscious of critiquing those aspects of the Bible that don't lend themselves to a multicultural church.

The political nature of the church and the way in which power was gained and shared was the focal point of the pastor's reflections as he moved to change the life of the church. He was aware that the old leadership group took great pride in their church and wanted to continue to give meaningful leadership and service. He found ways to engage these persons in conversation with the new group so that they would become more willing to share their power. He understood a multicultural ministry to be a place where major church decisions would be shared by all members of the congregation. This meant that the old group had to understand this more inclusive and democratic way of church leadership.

The church as a keeper of memories had to be honored but not allowed to circumscribe the development of new life for the church. Old church members were encouraged to discuss their old church's success as examples of what the church could be again. By bringing in a consultant who was trained in group process and diversity training they were at least able to identify how their experiences had shaped the memories and political orientations of the two groups. This was often an emotionally trying and painful process that was endured because of the mutual respect that the members gained from one another through their sharing and joint activities.

The language of music was also a key component in the revival of the church. The development of the Spirit choir in which the musical language of the African American and contemporary life were *the norm* would serve as another bridge toward transformation. Music was a non-threatening way of producing change as new and old members sang songs laced with a theological tradition of personal and social transformation.

The use of music is common in rites of passage activities. Music allows the development of a common orientation in a process that is inherently community building. It allows for instruction in conventional ways that are just as powerful as Bible studies or other structured lessons based on literacy and doctrines. Music as language goes beyond the learning of lyrics. It is a style that is fraught with deep theological meanings that extend into the emotional depths of the persons who sing and who participate in the worship service. This proved to be an important factor in the solidification of the church as a transformed multicultural body of believers.

Church #2—New Life

I want to lift up another church that also went through a transformation process. This is a predominantly African American church that had suffered some of the similar effects of the other churches I have been discussing. Black churches have also been affected by their class status in ways that are comparable to the ways in European American churches have been affected by race. Many hundreds of middle-class African American churches find themselves in old, city neighborhoods that were once thriving centers of the African American community. What was lacking in great wealth was made up by a sense of community and collective work and responsibility.

Long before the mega-church, it was not unusual for thousands to attend urban black churches in the major cities of this country. These churches were the products of the Great Black Migration from the South which swelled the black population of Northern, Eastern and Western cities alike. These churches became spiritual and social centers for African Americans who felt alienated as they moved from rural areas to life in the big cities.

These churches grew in wealth and prestige as their membership increased and their members gained educational advancement and social status. Most black professionals, either businessmen or those from the helping professions, like teachers, doctors and nurses were members of these churches. These churches allowed the poorest new immigrant to find a place next to the middle-class doctor or lawyer with little thought to social class, and those blacks who did not feel comfortable or welcomed by these churches simply formed their own or joined religious groups that were out of the mainstream. The early to mid-twentieth century was a time of tremendous growth and vitality of the black church and supplied the groundwork for the burgeoning, black middle-class that was to come.

The church I grew up in was a church like this. It was packed to the house on Sunday mornings with at least a thousand persons crowding into the church. There were Sunday night services at which visiting churches were entertained, Wednesday night services and even Friday Bible studies for the membership. There were many programs for youth and young adults and the choirs were alive with the latest gospel music. It was simply accepted that you would be a member of a church, the only question was which one you belonged to on any given Sunday.

Returning to the church twenty years later I would never know that this was the same church. As I joined my mother in the pew I found that the church was more than half empty and I recognized few, if any, of the adults who were my age that were still members in the church. This was true not only of my former church but of many of the churches in the area. Instead of European American flight, they had experienced another black migration to more affluent neighborhoods in different parts of the city and suburbs.

They were not running from any particular ethnic group, but were searching for the American dream of upward mobility and prosperity. As they attained middle-class status they moved out of the inner-city black ghetto for life in middle-class neighborhoods with better housing, schools and services. Some of the members continued to come to the church even though they no longer lived in the neighborhood. Without this solid core the church would have long ago closed its doors. They brought with them enough financial resources and numbers to keep the doors of the church open, but they had not developed a church ministry that would draw from their former neighborhoods, who were now peopled primarily by the forgotten black poor.

I will chronicle how one church dealt with this situation and by doing so lift up some of the theological and sociological factors in their recovery process.

Church J

Church J was located on the south side of a major American city. The neighborhood had gone through several transitions. It had once been an exclusive European American upper-middle-class neighborhood, but after the rapid social change of the 1960's and 70's it had moved quickly from being a predominantly European American ethnic neighborhood to becoming a predominantly black area.

The neighborhood is bordered and transected by several major city arteries. This gave the neighborhood a sense of life, not to mention busy streets and pollution from numerous trucks and cars on their way to other places in the region. There was a large indoor mall that had been erected when malls first came into fashion in American cities. Despite the European American flight it continued to exist for the neighborhood residents and other black community members who lived adjacent to the neighborhood. For those who couldn't or chose not to go shopping in the larger suburban malls this was an effective place to take care of business. Although the mall had lost much of its luster and its share of tenants and customers, its presence was a sign that the neighborhood continued to be viable.

The church had followed the patterns of most churches in the area. It had started as an all European American church and slowly incorporated a few black members as it made its transition from a European American to a black church. However, the church had the additional twist of imitating the European American church in its worship style. Its worship was staid and relatively lifeless which meant that it was also unattractive to black middle-class persons who still wanted to experience a sense of Spirit in their worship services. By the time of the mid-70's the church was down to a congregation of no more than forty persons and facing imminent death. It was then that it hired a part-time student pastor who began the daunting process of church revival on a grand scale.

Revival

Things began to change at the church almost immediately after the new pastor arrived. He was a highly-educated black minister who had definite ideas about the nature of the church and its relationship to the culture. For instance, he understood that the black church carried most of its theology in its music and he was therefore determined to improve the musical ministry of the church. As a trained musician himself he was especially well-equipped to lead this effort. He also searched for and found another talented gospel musician who was to become instrumental in building the music ministry of the church.

This church revitalization through music was a common strategy for church growth in the black community. I had many conversations regarding this topic with a female gospel musician who was instrumental in taking a small congregation of fifty persons to a church that is now over three thousand strong. The pastor of that church relied on her to use her musical abilities to reach persons who were not usually interested in normal church functions such as preaching and Bible study.

In the case of the church at hand the pastor and musician began by building a gospel chorus that would soon rival the more established musical groups in the city. This led to his church receiving instant credibility and visibility among the churches in his neighborhood and soon, throughout the city.

The pastor also understood that the black community had a strong affinity for "wordsmiths." Preachers, who in the words of Maya Angelou, "had music in their voices." He cultivated his preaching abilities until he was at a par with other pastors who had gained great popularity in the community. His sermons demonstrated his education through a thorough exegesis of biblical texts intermixed with how God could be of personal aid to persons in need. His strong storytelling ability was unusual in that he usually read from a lengthy script, something that most black preachers eschewed as a sign of oral weakness. Instead, he was able to make it work due to the strength of his storytelling and in-depth analysis of biblical and social situations.

It didn't take long for his church to grow in leaps and bounds and he soon built the first of several buildings that would house a bourgeoning congregation. As the church began to grow he also demonstrated exceptional leadership ability. He developed a special knack for delegating authority and involving talented and committed persons to commit their time and talents to the church. He challenged new members to serve in various areas of the church or to join in ongoing ministry activities. Every member was expected to participate in some form of ministry or study. The pastor challenged them to consider their cultural status as African Americans and their ethical responsibilities as Christians.

The pastor developed an African-centered theology that upheld the positive nature of African American heritage with a strong evangelical Protestant orthodox theology of salvation.

In a modified Niebuhrian topology he was developing a Christ and (sub) Culture paradigm, with a Christ against (dominant) Culture paradigm. In his paradigm he extolled the continuities between traditional African American values and traditional Christian virtues of pride, self respect, hard work, and so on. But he also recognized the negative ways in which the dominant culture had attempted to oppress the black community and so he preached against materialism and racism as major features of a culture that was anti-Christian.

His church was offering the black community a way of remaining true to its ethnic heritage while at the same time maintaining itself within the Protestant mode of social protest against injustice. He did not want the church to fall into its previous trap of becoming a church that was captive to its own class trappings, which meant that it would soon look down and separate itself from the black poor. Instead, by extolling black heroes and black culture he developed a religious philosophy that grounded itself in a black Christian liberation perspective.

His sermons were as insistent on the need for personal transformation as they were on criticizing the culture for its racist and consumerist attitudes. This kept the church grounded in a biblical perspective that was sublimely Christian. The church developed numerous Bible studies for all ages, many of whom were led or trained by the pastor himself. He also enlisted biblically trained pastors and teachers who would expand the ministry of the church by conducting Bible studies, retreats and seminars for the congregation on various days of the week.

One of the more remarkable features of the church was its appeal to young African American women. This was especially important since this church was growing at the same time that black women were reporting as being under greater social stress due to a lack of available black males for meaningful relationships. At the same time that the black female suicide rate was climbing, this pastor was enrolling thousands of African American women, who were finding a sense of home and identity in the Christian church. It's difficult to imagine a more impressive sight as one watches this church's main choir, which is composed of seemingly hundreds of mainly African American women, process into the sanctuary on Sunday mornings.

Perhaps the sight of thousands of black youth packed into the church during their summer youth revival and activities could rival this sight of a church that had come from the ashes of forty persons to a church membership of over 7,000 persons. The pastor's insistence on the importance of small group ministry had led to numerous ministries for children and families. There were athletic groups, academic groups, musical groups, and more, for children, youth and families.

Community Analysis

The pastor was successful in using the language of family to define the relationships of the church memberships. The church soon became modeled after an extended African family that had extensions all over one of the largest cities in the country. Church members developed a language that was unique to their understanding of the Christian gospel. They referred to themselves by the name of their church. They developed expectations of their church officials similar to those that one would expect of familial relations. The pastor was a father and mentor to children and young adults. He was a brother and friend to those of his age group and a favorite son to the older members of the church. Whether they were on the job at the post office or at the many public schools, members of the church went out of their way to recognize each other as members of the same extended church family.

Just as the language of family was important, so was the language of music. Music is often underrated as a form of communication, but since the advent of the Negro spiritual and even before that, when one examines the African religious past, music has played a central role in the life of African and African American religious communities. This church extended this understanding of the powerful role of music to include an awareness of the power of secular music as well.

It was not unusual for the church choirs to utilize the latest popular songs to communicate the Christian gospel. Words of popular love songs were replaced with Christian meanings as the church choirs turned popular songs into contemporary gospel music. The language of music also included dance as parishioners were encouraged to move and sway to the music in celebration of their faith. Young persons were encouraged to use hip hop or rap music in the service of communicating the message of the church. This became a community that was deeply embedded in the language of family and music.

The language of interpretation included the language of an African-centered faith. As stated before, there was a keen awareness of the relationship between the survival of black persons and the Christian faith. The ability to lift up the witness of blacks who were faithful to their community and their God was crucial in the formation of the identity of church members. This was especially important for the younger members of the church who consistently struggled with issues of race at their schools, places of employment and as victims of racial profiling. Many persons outside of the church in the European American community expressed fear of this part of the church's ministry. They confused black pride and self respect with hatred toward European Americans or the dilution of the Christian gospel. It took years to convince those persons that the church was solidly teaching the traditional Christian doctrines and that church officials had no need to fear that this was a Jonestown cult in the making.

These same church officials now lift up this church as a model for church revival as it is now the largest church in the denomination. The church has inspired dozens of persons to become engaged in Christian ministry. Its former members are productive in ministry and other professions throughout the country in various professional posts.

As a community of interpretation I have noted its stress on biblical literacy. There is also a general emphasis on education as a means of expressing Christian discipleship and as a means of attaining success. I am acquainted with one minister at the church who has taught the same weeknight Bible class for approximately twenty years. In this time he has developed a close pastoral relationship with his Bible study participants which serves to strengthen the family nature of the church.

Perhaps the stickiest part of the church's road to recovery was political. The pastor often found himself having to contend with lay leadership that did not always understand or embrace his vision. It became important to his success that he devoted his primary energy to the traditional roles of a pastor. In this case, teaching and preaching. He was able to enlist church members to serve as visitors to the sick and shut-ins, which was extremely important as the church began to grow to astronomical proportions. He weathered more than one storm by following closely the polity of the church which protected him from spurious charges. Without a thorough understanding of church rules and regulations it is doubtful that he would have been able to develop his ministry without undue interference.

The Church as Natural Community

The metaphor that these churches used the most in describing the operation of their churches was the metaphor of family. The church was not only the bride of Christ it was the family of God. The African American church in the United States has a long history of the use of family as its primary metaphor. Born out of slavery, it was as the noted scholar W.E.B. DuBois recognized, the first family for many African Americans who were not allowed to have the benefits of a natural family. The church became the place where everyone was thought to be related in a deeper spiritual sense that was even more important than natural bonds, although the natural family terms of mother, father, uncle, aunt, brother and sister were used to refer to members of the church and community.

The church stood as an ideal family for these congregations. In a time when talk show hosts, self-help books and numerous experts emphasize the dysfunctional characteristic of the modern family, these churches emphasize their respective churches as models of a functional family that operates on the basis of love and respect for its members. This is a tremendously attractive metaphor for the millions of Americans who feel their families threatened by an increasingly impersonal technological society.

The family metaphor helps to create a sense of identity for the church participants. The church as a natural community becomes responsible for overseeing the important rites of passage that all humans experience in community. From birth to death the church is responsible for giving its members a place where they can pass through the important events of their lives from baptism to burial. These churches made sure that they had adequate staff or programs to minister to their members in each stage of their life. The pastors had an entrepreneurial spirit in that they were willing to entertain the development of ministries that would provide the needed support for their members throughout the life cycle.

In my time at Old Church I was constantly amazed at how lightly the church leaders took their role in this capacity. Even though the church consultant and every church leader I spoke to understood that the church had lost members and were not gaining new members due to their failure to develop a viable church school program, little was done to correct this glaring difficulty. I even volunteered to staff the nursery if this would help to bring and keep new families in the church. The consultant's idea to sell some of the church's assets in order to hire a religious educator was ignored and this vital feature of the church's ministry was left to languish unfulfilled.

Without the presence of the young, the only natural events that could be celebrated were old age and death, a situation that becomes very depressing over time. Even the church itself was dim and lacking light, which led to a feeling of gloominess and despair. Suggestions to change the lighting were also placed on hold and one of the leaders expressed regret that he hadn't simply replaced the regular light bulbs with a more powerful lighting system when he had the chance several years ago.

I remember coming to Old Church after having taken my class to visit another church that was undergoing revitalization and renewal. I was amazed at how depressing it was to enter Old Church because of its lack of adequate lighting. The other church was built very much along the same lines as Old Church but the church was filled with bright banners and more than adequate lighting. The church leadership's failure to act on such a simple but needed change speaks to their sense of paralysis in the face of change.

The church as a natural community provides the members with a sense of identity. The rituals which accompany the natural stages of life: baptism, confirmation, marriage, discipleship, church membership, and death are important means by which the church instills in its members, or better yet, teaches its members the purpose of church membership. These rituals explain what the church member is supposed to believe as the individual grows and matures under the guidance of the church. A church that does not pay attention to the importance of this natural progression is in danger of losing opportunities to establish this sense of church identity.

These churches used small groups to attract and instruct new members. These members then became a part of the church's ministry as a natural community. They were inextricably linked in the churches that proved successful. The European American mega-church was peculiarly aware of the way in which the small group reinforced the ministry of the church. After being drawn into the church through Bible studies or other small group activities the new members were encouraged to express their identity to the church by placing themselves and their families under the rituals of the church. This often meant baptism or some kind of ritual declaration of faith.

Anthropologists have written reams regarding the importance of rites of passage of so-called primitive people. What we have often overlooked in our desire to be distinctive from Third World people is that the church is also primarily engaged in performing rites of passage for its membership and just as in the African or Oceanic tribes person, the Christian church person also gains his or her identity through the rituals of the church.

It is difficult for us to see how important those ritual times are, yet it is those rituals which have the most profound effects on our lives. They bind us one to the other and to the church as members of a human yet divine family. This is a family with a history. Like a family with a genealogy that has been influenced by its ancestors, the church also has a history which has helped to define its present. The ancestors of the church, whether we call them saints or founders, have helped to form the identity of the church. By telling their story during the most important ritual times of the church, whether it is in Sunday morning worship service or during times of instruction, these stories help to initiate us into the world of the church and of that particular church.

Stories of biblical heroes and heroines are a part of this formation process. Churches choose particular heroes that most fit their historical perspective. A church that emphasizes the Prophets will develop a different identity than one that emphasizes the letters of Paul, the apostle. African American churches have historically emphasized the Old Testament prophets and the birth narratives of Jesus of Nazareth to form a particular identity that leads to an attitude of Christ against or transformer of Culture. Evangelical Protestant churches have emphasized the New Testament writings of Paul the apostle to the Gentiles, whose major task in life and death was the proclamation of spiritual salvation to the non-Jewish world. These churches have been less interested in social transformation in favor of a theological and ethical stance that emphasized Christ.

In the churches I examined, biblical preaching was an important part of the church's ministry. Each pastor had a deep respect, almost love, for the biblical text. Whether they had a fundamentalist or more liberal theology they each made biblical preaching an important part of their ministry and work. Their preaching was important because of the central place that the worship service had on Sunday morning. Even though they were aware of the sociological factors that led to their church's growth they were also grounded in a belief that their ministry was a continuation of a biblical story. They saw themselves and their church as actors in a Christian drama whose story was not yet completed.

Their ability to convey this sense of participation to their congregation gave their churches an important sense of their own participation in the church. They were a part of something much bigger than themselves which gave them an inflated sense of their own importance. Inflated, not in a negative way, but in a sense that their actions would have an importance far beyond their present place and time. This gave their churches a sense of adventure and purpose and helped to bind the members as participants of a quest rather than members of a bureaucratic organization.

The rituals of the church reinforced their sense of being a human and natural community, yet one that was engaged in a higher sense of purpose. The common eating of bread and wine in which the congregation pledges their loyalty to the church's mission and purpose serves as a powerful human, yet divine, ritual of consecration. The use of the most plentiful and most necessary of all of the natural world's earthly resources, water, in the rituals of baptism or foot washing also produce a powerful sense of community among diverse persons from various walks of life. Experiencing these rituals remind the members of their own commitments and allow them to welcome others into the common life of the church.

The Church as Human Community

From the smallest church to the largest mega-church, each church understood the sociological implications of the church. They approached their church as a part of a larger social fabric and it was the nature of this fabric that they attempted to understand before developing their ministry. This took the form of in-depth sociological surveys conducted by church consultants and other professionals to having their church members canvass the neighborhood or filling out surveys about the community. These churches determined the social make-up of the immediate and surrounding neighborhoods to varying levels of sophistication. More importantly than the money spent on the survey or the use of outside consultants was the churches' attitudes toward the use of sociological information. Unlike Old Church, which took a relative disdain of consultation, these churches embraced the sociological information and made it an integral part of their church's strategy for ministry.

It is important that pastors and church leaders avoid an attitude of anti-intellectualism. As we saw with Old Church it can be a way of denying the gravity of the church's situation. The church may employ other strategies that can stifle the use of sociological information. Cost may be a factor in a church's refusal to deal with a church consultant. But I discovered that even with small churches on limited budgets, the successful churches were able to develop social information through informal means such as having small focus groups about the neighborhood or by passing out surveys in the church bulletin.

It was not the cost or expertise of the consultant that was important, instead it was the church's attitude toward the usefulness of the information. The use of an interim pastor in one of the churches helped to prepare the church to adopt a different attitude towards itself and the community. Self studies can be valuable aides, but once again, only if the church leadership is open to the data that is generated by the study. I am emphasizing the church's openness to new information because of the way in which this lack of psychological flexibility prevented Old Church from using its assets to develop an effective ministry.

The fact that the consultant wanted them to sell off assets that they had deemed precious and a part of their identity was a point of resistance that they could not overcome. A part of their assets involved extra acreage on the church site that the church was not using. I believe that this land, as well as the paintings, had become a part of the Old Guard's identity since the land and paintings had been acquired during their life at the church. The consultant and the pastor were unable to break down this psychological barrier and, as I have stated before, the church was unable to act on the consultant's recommendations.

The successful churches I analyzed all recognized the importance of the church as a community. Their ministry reflected this in that they emphasized small group interaction as an important process in their ministry. My time at a conservative seminary with denominational consultants emphasized the importance of small groups for church revitalization. Whereas the members of their growing congregations felt as though their emphasis on the Bible was the main reason for their growth, these denominational leaders recognized that in fact it was their development of small groups in which they carried out the Bible study that was producing the churches' growth.

These consultants recognized the human need for belonging that only a small group can provide. The first small group that any person encounters is the family. The family as a small group is essential for the development of a sense of belonging, identity, emotional comfort and sense of purpose. Even the largest mega-churches are organized by a proliferation of small groups. This was true of the large, black urban churches that developed numerous boards and organizations to the modern mega-churches that have small groups meet for study or ministry throughout the week.

This point cannot be overemphasized because it strikes at the heart of what it means to be in human community. People are fundamentally social beings. Church leaders that recognize this look for ways to develop small group interaction. The modern urban world is characterized by impersonal bureaucracies which leave the urban person thirsting for intimacy. This need is best met by the development of small groups with leaders who are good at encouraging persons to feel welcome and comfortable.

Old Church attempted to develop a Men's Group but it was too unstructured to produce the kind of intimacy that occurs in a small group that has identified its purpose. One reason why a family is effective is because its members are aware of its purpose and boundaries. The power of the small group has been recognized by contemporary sociologists of religion as absolutely essential for a healthy church.

The churches I examined as models of successful ministry involved one black mega-church, and a small to moderate-sized neighborhood church that was going through transition. They may have differed in ethnicity, size and geographic location but they all understood the importance of leadership and the development of small groups.

It would be safe to say that the pastors of these churches were open to sociological information that was pertinent for the ministry of their churches. They were seminary educated and lovers of the Bible and theological literature. They understood the expression that "people are human first." This meant that they had an acute appreciation of the human frailties of their members but they also had high expectations of their members.

CHAPTER 5

Should Your Church Live?

■■

THIS CHAPTER WILL PROVIDE CHURCHES with a series of questions that will reveal the cultural similarities and disparities between the church and its community. This will be an assessment tool that church leaders can use to discuss problem areas and areas of growth.

I hope that I have made my point regarding the necessity of a church understanding the relationship between culture and the life and ministry of a particular church. In this chapter I will provide questions and exercises for churches to conduct in order to gain information on their own theological and cultural perspective, and that of the culture within which they live and move and have their being. Whatever may have been said about the Apostle Paul it must be acknowledged that he was an excellent diagnostician of culture and how it related to his ministry. The same can be said for the pastors of churches that have made a successful transition from death to life.

Exercise One: Tour of the Neighborhood

The first thing I recommend for pastors and church leaders is that they take a tour of their neighborhood. This can take place as a walking tour, a driving tour, or now in these days of Cyberspace, a virtual tour. In fact, it may be an advantage if a church has the computer capacity to develop a virtual neighborhood of their community.

A walking tour can be conducted alone but it is preferable that it be conducted by the pastor and other church leaders.

The pastor may want to conduct a preliminary tour by him or herself in order to get a lay of the land and familiarize themselves with the high and low points of the neighborhood. I believe that it is important for the church to claim the neighborhood in which it is situated. Churches must develop a proprietary attitude towards its community so that it feels responsible for the well-being of its community. This may be done in concert with other churches once a church feels strong enough to move outside of its borders, but regardless it is a necessary attitude to have if a church is interested in transformation. Before one can seek or plan for transformation it must first come to know what or who needs transformation.

I have never ceased to be surprised what can happen or what contacts can be made on this walking tour. It establishes a church's presence in the neighborhood in an immediate way that is superior to other forms of communication. This is especially true of city neighborhoods that provide easy access to dense neighborhoods. This is also important for more suburban neighborhoods as well. Church leaders will be surprised at what events can occur when the church leaders walk the local mall to introduce the church to its occupants. Churches must lose their shyness regarding their "right" to visit with persons in their neighborhoods. Many of the persons in Old Guard had a kind of shyness or fear of being seen as too intrusive by the community. I would offer that the community in most cases is ready to welcome the ministry of the church but they often feel as though a church and its membership is unapproachable and distant, especially if many of those members are not living in the neighborhood. This is a revival of the old concept of the parish being a geographic space where a church is expected to minister to the needs the community.

I have had many remarkable and memorable experiences during these walking tours. I have had encounters with persons from new religious movements and wound up in dialogue over our similarities and differences on busy street corners. I have seen the despair of persons whose only place of residence is a dilapidated crack house or dingy apartment. These encounters help to spread the news that the church is open and available to the needs of persons in the community. I have found that word quickly spreads that the church is interested in the community and the community responds in kind.

It is also possible to conduct driving tours of the community. In this situation a pastor or other church leaders can make use of the expertise of persons who are long-time residents of the community or even public officials. Many police stations offer public-minded citizens the opportunity to ride with police officers as they make their rounds. There are also community relations specialists with many police or fire departments that can be enlisted in this effort. New pastors should take advantage of these community practitioners and make the church known as a place that may be able to provide assistance to persons in need.

Universities can also be helpful in this effort. Many departments of sociology provide tours of various neighborhoods to its new students. It is possible to invite those professors to provide similar tours for church leaders at minimal or no cost since public service is required of most university professors.

With the advent of advanced computer modeling it is also possible that city and university professors have information about the community that can be of use to the church. One such project at my present university has coded the housing resources of each city neighborhood so that it is possible to discover the kind and condition of every house in that community. Housing information is extremely important as a social indicator of communities. They can tell the church a great deal about the needs of persons that are affected by particular housing conditions. All of this information is on a computer database and can be accessed on the web. Professors are also willing to consult with communities that are experiencing distress as a normal part of their work.

Questions:

1. What do you anticipate finding on your tour of the neighborhood?

2. What is the nature of the housing stock in your community? Are they mainly apartments or single homes? What needs distinguish home from apartment dwellers? Is the development of adequate housing a need for this community?

3. Who did you meet on your tour? Were they aware of your church? Have they ever been personally touched by the ministry of your church?

4. Who went with you on your tour? Did you agree or disagree about what you experienced on the tour? What differences of observation or need arose during your tour?

5. How do you feel your church fits into the neighborhood? Is your church of similar ethnic or socio-economic background or are there large disparities? How did you feel as you talked to persons from different social backgrounds? Do you think you made any personal contacts with people in the community?

6. How did the tour affect your view of the church's role in the community? Did any new ministry ideas come to light? What can you do to follow up these new findings?

Exercise Two: Socio-Religious Analysis

Churches should assess their theological and ethical orientations. I have put forth Neibuhr's categories as a way of understanding these differing orientations. It is extremely important for the church leadership to understand its theological and ethical orientation. It may be that the church leaders are not aware of how their theological positions are affecting their ability to minister to their community. Churches who are heavily involved in a Christ and Culture stance have very little motivation or need to reach persons in their neighborhood. Unconsciously, they have become ambassadors for the culture. This is fine as long as there is continuity between the church and its community. However, once the community changes, the church is left with a cultural stance that is out of touch with its community. Transformation is impossible without some adjustment of the church's ethical orientation. It must seek to be transformed from within before it can engage in transformation outside of the church.

Categories:

How does your church see itself in relationship to the dominant culture?

Christ of Culture—Assimilationist Model

1. Does your church see itself as an extension of the cultural expressions found in the culture?

2. Are the values of the country the values of the church?

3. Does it have an "America: love it or leave it" attitude?

4. Does it understand the multicultural nature of the American public?

5. Does it involve or celebrate other cultures or classes of people?

If your church answers "yes" to the first three questions and "no" to the last two, then it is showing signs of a Christ of Culture model.

Christ against Culture—Oppositional Model

1. Does your church finds itself at odds with the dominant cultural expressions?

2. Does your church's values contradict those of the culture?

3. Does your church spend most of its time distinguishing itself from the dominant culture?

4. Does your church provide a safe haven from the world?

5. Does your church offer a way of life that is "in but not of the world"?

If your church answers "yes" to these questions, then it is reflective of a Christ against Culture model.

Christ Transformer of Culture—Transformational Model

1. Does your church see itself at odds with the culture?

2. Does your church attempt to change the culture?

3. Does your church believe that the culture can be transformed?

4. Does your church find ways to involve itself with diverse people and parts of the culture?

5. Does your church integrate diverse peoples and attitudes in its leadership?

If your church answers "yes" to these questions, then it is reflective of a Christ the Transformer of Culture model.

After this survey is taken by members of the church or church leadership the responses should be discussed and the implications for the life of the church addressed. For churches that are in states of negative growth the underlying question that has to be answered has to do with the church's willingness to change its means of relating to the community and its ability to share power and include diverse populations. At this time the church may want to do a more in-depth sociological analysis of its community habits and practices. Once again, Gustafson's model may prove helpful here.

Exercise Three: Church Community Analysis— Human Community

1. What are the important rituals that your church engages in? (Communion, Baptism, Confirmation, Marriage, Funerals.)

2. How does the performance of these rituals shape the life of your church?

3. Which rituals have had the most prominence in the last few years?

4. What does this have to say about the state of your church?

5. Is there anything unique about the way your church conducts its rituals?

6. Who in the church participates in these rituals?

7. Are there ways in which others can be involved in this important facet of the church?

Community of Language and Interpretation

1. How would you describe the religious language of your church? Is it liberal, conservative, fundamentalist, evangelical?

2. What role does the Bible and Bible study play in the life of your church? Is it of central importance or only used on occasion?

3. Does a person have to be highly educated to be a member of your congregation? How does the language of the church reflect its social status?

4. What role does music play in the life of the church? Who is involved in the ministry of music? Does it have a high level of importance in the church?

5. What values or orientations are reflected in the music? Is it mainly traditional hymns and anthems? Does the music reflect contemporary or diverse musical traditions?

Community of Politics

1. What is the political structure of your church? Is it congregational or connected by a church hierarchy?

2. What is the political structure in the individual congregation? Who is involved in the leadership of the church?

3. How would you describe the selection of church leadership? Is it an open or closed process?

4. How often does the church leadership share with the congregation at large? Are decisions made in the open or are they the responsibility of the few?

5. Is your church open to diverse leadership by class, gender, age and ethnicity? What would be an ideal leadership structure?

CHAPTER 6

Observations for a Successful Ministry

∷

THIS FINAL CHAPTER WILL INTRODUCE you to my experience as a director of a project that was designed to get the middle-class church involved in the lives of poorer members of its community. In a time when faith-based organizations, including and especially the churches, are being looked to for providing needed social services to the poor and disenfranchised these programs that were developed in this project may be of help to those churches who wish to play a greater role in ministry to the least and last in their community.

I became involved in the project as a doctoral student at the University of Chicago Divinity School. I had spent the previous two years as a Campus Minister with the Methodist and other Protestant religious groups, working particularly close with the Disciples and United Church of Christ ministries. Always the advocate for racial and gender justice, I helped to develop the anti-apartheid campaign with sympathetic students, staff and professors, and like my political activities at the Pacific School of Religion, this often meant an encounter with the powers that ran these institutions.

In seminary I helped to develop a prayer and study group around the sermons of Martin Luther King Jr. This group eventually led a protest on campus over the unfair firing of several women of color who were caught in the seminary's decisions to downsize its staff. It was my first experience at seeing the ways in which a racist ideology can erode the good intentions of European American Christians. Although the

106 Can This Church Live?

protest began with over forty students in solidarity, the demonstration which led to a confrontation with the administration was supported by only five students. The original European American students had undergone what King called "the paralysis of analysis" and were more concerned with their future prospects than the injustices at hand. The last meeting we held was dominated by students, primarily adults in their late twenties and thirties, who expressed how they were more in need of a party than a planning session to help the women who were being wronged. I learned the hard way that it is not only the so-called conservatives who had a problem in the implementation of social justice.

Perhaps the proudest moment in my university career happened during the granting of my Ph.D. degree by the President of the University of Chicago, Dr. Hanna Gray. Dr. Gray was known as a tough administrator who was also honored by Ronald Reagan for her political views. I had gone toe-to-toe with Ms. Gray over racial profiling issues on campus and so we had a history of confrontation. I must say that Dr. Gray responded to our issues and dealt effectively with the campus policemen who were guilty of racist practices. During the awarding of my degree I wondered if Dr. Gray would remember me since it had been six years since I left the campus. When my name was called and I went to receive my degree, Dr. Gray said, "Congratulations Reverend Matthews." Her acknowledgment of my role as a minister and scholar gave me hope that the European American and black community could work together in an air of mutual respect even when confrontation is necessary.

I left my role as a Campus Minister in order to develop a joint project that was sponsored by the Chicago Theological Seminary and the Carnegie Corp. of New York. As I stated before, this project was meant to help churches become more effective in their ministry to low-income families, in this case, the black community. After I was hired, I helped complete the specifications for the grant and was the Project Director for the three-year life of the grant. In the following paragraphs I want to report and discuss what we discovered because it is important for those churches who want to be a living entity in their communities.

We began the project by contacting numerous churches who wanted assistance in developing ministry programs in their communities. We would be able to provide them with a seminarian intern who could work with the church for 10-20 hours/week, including preparation and transportation time. We also provided the churches with approximately $2,000/year for use of church space and programmatic support. We stipulated that each church had to have the support of the pastor and be able to identify three to five laypersons that would serve as a planning and oversight committee and work directly with the seminarian.

The churches we chose were middle-class churches in some of the poorest economic areas of the city. These churches and laypersons had chosen to remain in these neighborhoods although many of their members had moved to other more financially stable parts of the city. The children of these members had also either moved out of these neighborhoods or, in many cases, out of the city as well. The persons in the community were poorer than the church members and felt ostracized and unwelcome in a church where they did not have the same access to wealth and education, among other things.

We discovered that the laypersons in the church wanted desperately to aid their more needy brothers and sisters. There was very little condescension or snobbery among the laypersons toward the community. But they had very little in terms of resources like second staff members or ministry professionals who could develop and implement plans for ministry. We found that there was very little sense of abandoning the black poor among these middle-class blacks. In fact, many of them worked with poorer black children and families as teachers, nurses, social workers, and so on. What we did find was that these laypersons, who were predominantly female, and the pastors, who were predominantly male, seldom sought each other's counsel as they went about their work and/or ministry. This meant that they were unable to make use of each other's vast knowledge of expertise and resources in developing a coordinated ministry approach. Gender roles are often overlooked as a reason why a church is not effectively ministering to its community. Pastors and other church leaders must remain sensitive to the insight that female members can make in the identification of ministry needs and possibilities.

The first observation then is that a successful program was dependent on the commitment and vision of laypersons, women and men, who were willing to meet with church and social service professionals in the planning and implementation of ministry programs.

The second observation that was just as necessary as the first was that a successful program was dependent on the pastor's involvement. The more contact or approval the pastor gave to the ministry group's efforts the more likely it was to succeed. What this alludes to is a point that was made previously, i.e., effective leadership is the key to effective ministry. Pastors and laypersons who had solid ethical and theological grounding in their determination to develop inclusive ministries were the most successful. In fact, we began with ten churches but cut the number by five for the second and third years of the project because, one or the other of these leadership components were missing.

The third observation is important in the midst of this debate about government support of faith-based organizations. We discovered that even though the churches were grateful for the financial support they were also leery of becoming too dependent on outside sources of revenue. Churches, and the black church in particular, have long taken pride in their ability to remain free of governmental and other outside influences. Anything that might sacrifice their independence is looked at with a wary eye.

These programs developed from a sense of communal trust with a minimum of direct outside help. We found that consultants who understood the community and its particular neighborhoods were helpful in giving churches vital demographic information that could be used to plan particular programs. One social worker who was an expert in teen pregnancy in low-income black neighborhoods was important for one church group in their development of a teen pregnancy prevention program. This church was located in an area of the city that had the highest teen pregnancy rate in the city and several of the laypersons involved in the program had been teen mothers.

The seminarian and laypersons were so successful in developing their program based on information gained from social agencies, helping professionals, and church religious education materials that they developed a program in which none of the girls involved became pregnant. Not only was their goal achieved but the group of girls they worked with became active participants in the life of the church and formed a nucleus for a youth group, both male and female, for other young persons in the community.

A fourth observation was that effective conflict management was an important necessity in the early stages of the program.

We found that at least a period of three to six months was necessary for working out the numerous issues that arose from the process of group formation. Many of the laypersons expressed a need for ministry themselves before they could minister to others. We found that spiritual and social support was necessary in the form of Bible study, prayer, or workshops with religious or social service professionals.

Just because laypersons may have been in the same church for years doesn't mean that they really know or trust one another. Persons may become involved in ministry in order to fulfill a need that has gone unfulfilled. An extended time of reflection and prayer was foundational for the development of these ministry teams. It was important not to jump too quickly to the development of specific ministries before the teams could bond as a group.

Finally, we also discovered it was important to allow the groups to grow in unexpected ways. Programs that began with one particular emphasis often experienced a mushrooming effect which led to the inclusion of other program areas and age groups. For instance, one church wanted to start a sewing group for ten to fifteen neighborhood girls and wound up with a scouting program that enrolled close to a hundred children.

Profile in Ministry

It might be helpful to follow the example of one church in its development of a community ministry program. One of the churches decided to develop a support group for young adults as its ministry program. The group met each Wednesday evening in one of the larger meeting rooms in the church. The church is located in a community with extremes in terms of income and social class. One neighborhood in the community may be extremely poor with lots of subsidized housing and it may be adjacent to an extremely wealthy neighborhood with Tudor and Victorian-style mansions. This community had undergone racial transition and was now struggling to maintain a sense of economic and racial stability.

The participants in the support group were reflective of this economic range. There were lower-income persons who were struggling to keep their families clothed and sheltered, and there were established, middle-class professionals. One of the members of the group had been awarded a fellowship at one of the elite universities in the area as one of the city's teachers of the year. The previous pastor of this predominantly black church was a European American male who had suffered an unexpected and tragic death. The church was still in the process of mourning, and under the guidance of the new pastor was attempting to establish the ministry role it felt called to play in relationship to the community. The church also sponsored a day care center and allowed a state-sponsored day care to rent some of its space.

The group began with six adults, primarily consisting of the seminarian, pastor and the three sponsoring laypersons. After a year the average adult attendance was twenty participants. Several of the parents also brought their children to the weekly support meetings which swelled the group by six to ten participants. In the early stages of the program, the seminarian led the group in discussions concerning the history of the black church, using a film strip and study guide from the UCC publishing house. The seminarian felt that by giving the church a sense of its ethnic history the members seemed to be galvanized for ministry and it answered many of their questions concerning their identity as members of a predominantly black church.

After several weeks the group members determined that they needed to develop more trust and so they decided to use a study program called "Building Up One Another." Different participants were asked to lead sessions throughout the year and the seminarian and pastor also led special sessions designed to increase trust including gestalt exercises, foot washing ceremonies, etc.

On a night that I attended the support group I found the members to be responsive to the leadership of the pastor and seminarian. They expressed a desire to be more effective witnesses in their community but were still uncertain about specific ministry projects that they wanted to develop. However, they all wanted to continue meeting as a group that lent its support to one another. One member, a young single parent, expressed her gratitude to the group for giving her emotional support when she was in search for employment. She was eventually successful in her job quest and she expressed her thanks for the group being there for her during her time of need.

From listening to this group it became obvious that the more socially successful persons were serving as role models for those persons who were lifting themselves from poverty. There was a sense of mutual love and concern for one another that permeated the speech and attitude of the group. The group continued to meet for the duration of the life of the program and members of the group gradually became involved in other aspects of the church's ministry. The day care center became an important focus for the group and several members of the group began to work with other helping professionals to increase the level of education for the parents of the children in the day care center.

This church serves as an example of several of the points that were made previously. The leadership of the clergy and laypersons was essential for the success of the group. This is an example of a group that originally wanted to develop ministries for the community but soon found that they had needs themselves that needed to be attended to before they were prepared to venture out to the community. By looking inward they found that they became the objects of their own ministry and they wound up attracting other adults who also felt the fragmentation of life in the urban core.

What was important is that they were inclusive of all kinds of persons in their community. Differences of class or race were not barriers for the constitution of the group. Their vision of the Kingdom of God and the church as a place that was inclusive regardless of social status allowed their group to grow and prosper. As they met the spiritual needs of the group through prayer, Bible study, historical and social studies they found themselves enriched and formed closer bonds. This group eventually became important in establishing other forms of ministry but it was first important to build up one another. Their experience in the group meant that they also built up their ability to function in relationship to other persons who were in need. The group became a living embodiment of the principles of inclusion and compassion.

This profile also showed how little outside money was necessary for the development of the group. The seminarian interns were paid a three thousand dollar stipend, and a fifteen hundred dollar grant for financial aid. This meant that the pastor now had a trained, or in this case, an "in-training" professional to help develop the project. The cost for study materials was minimal. Many churches should be investing in extra personnel when a downward slide begins, and instead they become protective of every penny when a few well spent dollars can reap huge dividends.

This church was also very leery of applying for federal money for its day care center. They did not want to be prevented from providing a religious-based educational program for the children in their center due to the separation of church and state. Churches are in the business of teaching values based on their religious stories. Government regulations that prevent them from relaying this information to the clients they serve challenge the very purpose of the existence and effectiveness of faith-based institutions.

Conclusion

■

As a doctoral student taking classes in Anthropology at the University of Chicago, I quickly became aware that the oppressed of a community rarely have the opportunity or the leisure to study the oppressive or dominant community. This fact is a part of the dynamics of oppression. In Hegelian terms, the slave seldom gets to study and write about the master. In this book I am attempting to reverse these roles. I am a professor of African American religion and culture who is writing about European American religion and culture. Instead of writing yet another work on the black religious experience, which I and many of my black colleagues have done, it is also important to write about the experiences of race and racism of the European American churches whose members continue to support a racially-segmented society.

The question that Gandhi posed to Howard Thurman is still alive. The Christian church has yet to prove it has the ability to transform its race-based structural organization. Self interest by blacks and European Americans may be a reason why this continues to be the case in the 21st century. One community has a legacy of power gained through its racially exclusive policies and the other community having to succeed under the terms of European American exclusion does not want to risk being assimilated by a European American whole that has little sympathy for its distinct history.

Both sides must come to grips with the continually evolving social situation in which racial diversity will be the word of the future. Churches begun as racial enclaves are only as strong as the social moment allows. More importantly, churches that are built on racially-exclusive principles are built on a foundation that is not true to the message of Christianity that proclaims the ultimate equality of all persons under God. We may labor in racially-colored gardens but these gardens were not built by the Master Gardener. Instead, the sins of slavery and discrimination are the architects and the Christian church continues to meet each Sunday with little awareness of the need for urgent change.

The Christian church should be at the forefront of social and political change if that is what is necessary to produce churches that are not racial enclaves. Neighborhoods that are segregated should be the recipient of the ministry of churches that challenge its members to remain and not flee when the neighborhoods become racially diverse. Churches should consciously plan for racial inclusiveness just as it consciously plans for any other of its ministry programs. Partnerships can be formed with churches who have successfully navigated the racial divide and plans made to include cultural diversity as a principle of community building. This oldest of Christian sins must die a planned death by committed leadership who have an inclusive vision of the church. If this book helps those churches to live out that vision, then it will not have been a futile exercise.

A key question that the reader should ask is an old one that gets asked about many different human abilities. In this case, since the key to the revival of these churches has been the quality of the leadership, the question becomes: "Are leaders born or made?" The churches seem to have answered this question implicitly on the side of leaders being born to the task of leadership. The curriculum in theological schools would tend to affirm this position that leaders cannot be the object of formation. Seminaries and divinity schools seldom offer classes in leadership. There is the idea that the future minister must possess some obvious leadership skills or else they wouldn't be in the theological school preparing for ministry.

My experience in these settings would tend to argue for the opposite interpretation. Most of the seminarians I was acquainted with come to the ministry with muddled ideas of what it means to be an effective religious leader. The fortunate ones were taken under the wing of an effective leader and learned some of the principles of leadership from their mentor. Even so, this often produced a kind of "clone syndrome" in which the minister trainee sought to blindly imitate the gifts and graces of their mentor without having their mentor's abilities. They were blind to their own strengths and weaknesses as they attempted to teach like their pastor, or in other ways imitate the strengths of their minister. This sometimes meant that they would also imitate their mentor's weaknesses and/or vices. This can often have tragic consequences or give the trainee a false identity that becomes painfully obvious when the person becomes involved in a ministry setting that doesn't have all the resources that the senior minister took a lifetime to build. This can lead to a sense of inadequacy in the minister that is often hard to shake, which in turn negatively influences future ministerial opportunities.

Effective leadership as seen in the examples cited above in the text makes it clear that leadership is first of all dependent on the development of a vision that is theologically and ethically consistent with the church as a space and place that is inclusive of the diversity that presents itself to the church. This vision of the church stands as in the vision of secular leadership talk, a mission statement that the church then uses to build a strategic plan. The development of a concise understanding of the mission statement and strategic plan is the result of intense interaction between the pastor and lay leaders of the church.

This leads to the development of a leadership group that may include persons who are not presently in official leadership capacities of the church. However, the group models by its vision and its composition the direction that the church intends to support as it opens itself to the community. It is amazing how diversity itself lends a dynamic to church growth. As persons of disparate backgrounds come together they activate a sense of newness and excitement that is akin to the excitement of the initial Pentecost experiences. Persons grow as they become open to other cultural experiences and more importantly to persons of different cultures. Instead of the routine and expected, the church begins to experience the heady wine of new experiences as persons who are committed to the same vision become partners in the ministry and life of the church.

It is also important to restate how important small groups are for the life of these churches. Small groups have the virtue of being entry places for new persons that are not as intimidating as the larger or more impersonal worship experiences. It is in the context of the small group that persons find the kind of spiritual and emotional support that they need to function in a highly impersonal society that is based on the goals of capitalist production. Churches are still the places that people look to for solace and a sense of companionship in a world that is beset by economic troubles, business failures, terrorist scares and the rest of the everyday dangers that go with life in a highly technical, urban society. Churches that develop opportunities for small group participation allow for the church to be a place with boundaries that can be easily broached by community members who are searching for a social space that is welcoming and challenging at the same time.

The life of the church is dependent on its willingness to allow for regular transfusions of new blood in its system. Help the church live by expanding its social borders and challenging its members to be models of a social reality that has yet to be achieved by the overwhelming majority of churches in the United States. Churches based on inclusiveness will have difficulties, but the answer to their difficulties will be in the problem itself. We must learn how to live with difference for the greater purpose of God and the church as it was intended to be.

Epilogue

The verdict is finally in. Instead of forcibly closing the three churches and merging them into a new church, the three churches were asked to vote their assent to the merger by the denominational officials. Old Church and its close ally voted for the merger with one negative vote from each congregation. The church built on the homogeneous principle demonstrated its different viewpoint by one third of its members voting against the plan. The three churches have yet to decide which buildings will remain, whether to build a new church, and a myriad of other issues. However, now that the merger is official the church begins the task of reformation with the aid of a consultant who will attempt to guide them through the process of change and transformation.

The three churches have had and continue to have the benefit of local, regional and national consultants. One national consultant stated that Old Church had the best facilities but had been doing the least in ministry. He also recommended that the property be sold since the church has never been able to grow in its present location. However, he realizes that it may be difficult to get Old Church members to participate in a new church start and as he put it "come out of their little pocket in the south part of the city to join the consolidated ministry." He recommended that all the properties be sold and that a church be started near the highway that would be visible and lead to the development of a regional ministry.

One can only wonder if the leaders of Old Church and the other churches have truly learned the lessons of their previous shortcomings. Will it open itself to the community in a way that is inclusive, healthy and empowering? Or will it attempt to live out a past dream of homogeneity and exclusivity? Only time and the quality of the leadership will tell. Judging from the new church's bulletin, one of the first tasks will be the election of new lay leadership.

I wonder if they realize just how crucial their selection will be to the life of their new church and its ministry. In my observations of their church and other churches this is certainly the key to any church that develops a ministry of personal and social transformation. May God grant them wisdom as they proceed on their journey.

Index

[decorative mark]

Other books from The Pilgrim Press:

■■

The Mark of Zion
Congregational Life in Black Churches

Stephen C. Rasor and Michael I. N. Dash
Foreword by Carl S. Dudley

Rasor and Dash propose that the black experience in America offers a significant presence in the religious landscape of contemporary society. In rural, urban, storefronts—as well as mega-churches—African American congregations foster an inward journey of spiritual growth and an outward journey of community outreach. The authors believe all churches must claim and/or reclaim this symbiotic journey. A profile of black churches is provided. This is the companion book to *The Shape of Zion: Leadership and Life in Black Churches* by Michael I. N. Dash and Christine Chapman.

ISBN 0-8298-1576-7/paper/144 pages/$16.00

The Shape of Zion
Leadership and Life in Black Churches

Michael I. N. Dash and Christine Chapman
Foreword by Lawrence H. Mamiya

The Shape of Zion is a practical and functional resource which provides a public profile of the organizational backbone of black congregations within the United Methodist Church and the Presbyterian Church (U.S.A.), and historically black congregations. Research for this resource was initiated to enhance the capability of religious denominations in the use of congregational studies. It includes questions for reflection, decision, and action.

ISBN 0-8298-1491-4/paper/208 pages/$19.00

The Indispensable Guide for Smaller Churches

David R. Ray

This book compliments Ray's earlier titles on smaller churches published by The Pilgrim Press: *The Big Small Church Book* (1992) and *Wonderful Worship in Smaller Churches* (2000). Ray expands on the earlier works by treating such subjects as communal theology, theories, and tools to understand smaller churches in worship, education, and finance. His vision is to lead smaller churches to the year 2030!

ISBN 0-8298- 1507-4/paper/320 pages/$24.00

Challenging the Church Monster
From Conflict to Community

Douglas J. Bixby

Bixby discusses the ways in which churches can restructure themselves and work through issues that are causing stagnation, early dismissal of pastors, and other conflicts that detract from the mission and vision of the church. Suggestions are offered for new ways to function so that mission and ministry can once again become priorities, and people can begin to feel their time and energy are being used for something other than adding fuel to the fire of conflict within the congregation.

ISBN 0-8298-1506-6/paper/128 pages/$16.00

The Generation Driven Church
Evangelizing Boomers, Busters, and Millennials

William and Le Etta Benke

The Benkes seek to revitalize the ministries of small and mid-size churches by helping them to adjust to the changing culture. It also offers strategic approaches that will re-orient ministries to attract younger generations and take churches with an "inward focus," (churches devoid of conversion growth because of the absence of meaningful outreach to un-churched adults who comprise the post-modernist cultures) to an "outreach focus."

ISBN 0-8298-1509-0/paper/128 pages/$13.00

Behold I Do a New Thing
Transforming Communities of Faith

C. Kirk Hadaway

Recent talk and thinking about congregations concentrating on declining church attendance. Author Kirk Hadaway thinks an important part of the conversation is missing—how can churches, in spite of the decline, remain engaged in the mission of transforming lives? Looking at churches in new ways and holding new expectations will allow church leadership to guide congregations in the journey where transformation and renewal is constant and embraced.

ISBN 0-8298-1430-2/paper/160 pages/$15.00

How To Get Along with Your Church
Creating Cultural Capital for Ministry

George B. Thompson Jr.

This resource incorporates Thompson's research and observations on pastoring a church. He finds that the pastors who are most successful in engaging their parishioners are the ones who develop "cultural capital" within their congregations, meaning that they invest themselves deeply into how their church does its work and ministries.

ISBN 0-8298-1437-X/paper/176 pages/$17.00

Futuring Your Church
Finding Your Vision and Making It Work

George B. Thompson Jr.

This resource allows church leaders to explore their congregation's heritage, its current context, and its theological bearings. Dr. Thompson provides insights that enable church members to discern what God is currently calling the church to do in this time and place. It is a practical, helpful tool for futuring ministry.

ISBN 0-8298-1331-4/paper/128 pages/$14.95

The Big Small Church Book

David R. Ray

Over sixty percent of churches have fewer than seventy-five people in attendance each Sunday. *The Big Small Church Book* contains information on everything from practical business matters to spiritual development. Clergy and lay leaders of big churches can learn much here as well.

ISBN 0-8298-0936-8/paper/256 pages/$15.95

Legal Guide for Day-to-Day Church Matters
A Hand Book for Pastors and Church Leaders

Cynthia S. Mazur and Ronald K. Bullis

This book belongs on every pastor's desk because the church is not exempt from the growing number of lawsuits filed each year. The authors are clergy as well as attorneys.

ISBN 0-8298-0990-2/paper/148 pages/$6.95

To order these or any other books from The Pilgrim Press, call or write to:

The Pilgrim Press
700 Prospect Avenue East
Cleveland, OH 44115-1100

Phone orders: 1-800-537-3394 • Fax orders: 216-736-2206

Please include shipping charges of $5.00 for the first book and $0.75 for each additional book.

Or order from our Web sites at
www.thepilgrimpress.com and www.ucpress.com.

Prices subject to change.